17 designs in **Cashsoft**
Baby DK & **Cashcotton DK**
by Martin Storey

Welcome to Classic Bambino, the second RYC Classic brochure especially for your precious tots and adorable babies where we bring you bundles of energy full of suppressed giggles.

A new baby is such a joy and as they grow that joy turns into timeless memories. What better way to celebrate their early years than with one of these beautiful patterns.

There is a kind of romance to nursery rhymes that I have always found a great source of inspiration. Translating childhood images into garments and toys is a delight. For this brochure our chosen setting of a sweet shop shows off the collection perfectly bringing the atmosphere to life.

Traditional designs are complemented by contemporary shapes – slipovers for boys, a cape and a ballet wrap for girls. You will find cosy blanket for afternoon naps and the perfect faithful friends, Clarissa Cat, Derek Dog or Daphne Duck.

Cashsoft Baby was specially developed for RYC children's patterns not only because it is a pleasure for you to knit and soft enough for a baby's skin, but also because the range of colours are modern classics that work together in every combination.

Classic Bambino – a pleasure to knit, a garment to treasure.

Martin

Classic Bambino has a variety of patterns for babies and toddlers. Whether you are a new knitter or an experienced hand, there is something for everyone. These patterns are a celebration of childhood; the innocence and the energy all wrapped up in your love.

Diddle, diddle, dumpling, my son, John,
Went to bed with his trousers on,
One shoe off and one shoe on!
Diddle, diddle, dumpling, my son, John!

Bobby – a happy stripy hooded cardigan with a raglan sleeve and button through front.
Knitted in Cashsoft Baby DK, shown here in Crocus, Horseradish & Cloud. Pattern instructions page 46

Bo-peep – a feast of colour and texture, this simple striped raglan is embroidered and embellished with pastel coloured buttons.

Knitted in Cashsoft Baby DK, shown here in Borage, Pixie & Horseradish. Pattern instructions page 58

Tommy – this lovely chunky cable slipover is set off beautifully with a back ground of moss stitch.

Knitted in Cashcotton DK, shown here in Wheat. Pattern instructions page 48

Miss Muffet – this moss stitch cape has slits for little hands
and a rib yoke detail. Perfect for sitting on your tuffet.

Knitted in Cashsoft Baby DK, shown here in Borage. Pattern instructions page 56

Wiggly scarf – a riot of colourful zigzags finished off with fluffy pompoms

Knitted in Cashsoft Baby DK, shown here in Pixie & Cloud.
Pattern instructions page 63

Ring a-round the roses,
A pocket full of posies,
Atishoo, Atishoo! We all fall down!

Stripy – a vintage stripey polo shirt with an easy collar

Knitted in Cashsoft Baby DK, shown here in Blue Boy, Horseradish & Cloud.
Pattern instructions page 50

Polly, put the kettle on,
Polly, put the kettle on,
Polly, put the kettle on,
We'll all have tea.

Polly – a gorgeous short-sleeved ballet wrap which ties at the back and is decorated with a delightful picot edging.

Knitted in Cashcotton DK, shown here in Framboise. Pattern instructions page 60

'I'm Derek the dog and I love to scamper will you be my friend?'
'My name is Mr Sleepy Ted and I like a cuddle at bedtime.'

Both knitted in Cashsoft Baby DK, Mr Sleepy Ted [left] shown here in Crocus & Blue Boy, Derek dog [right] shown here in Horseradish. Pattern instructions page 68 & 66

Boatman – this charming fairisle slipover has a delightful all over boat motif.

Knitted in Cashsoft Baby DK, shown here in Cloud, Blue Boy, Horseradish & Limone. Pattern instructions page 54

Apple tree blanket [shown with Derek dog opposite] – a beautifully soft cot
blanket with an apple tree cable design worked in squares.

Knitted in Cashsoft Baby DK, shown here in Chicory. Pattern instructions page 64

Bow-wow – children holding hands and friendly dogs are the delightful motifs on this sweet sweater which buttons up the back.

Knitted in Cashsoft Baby DK, shown here in Horseradish, Crocus & Blue Boy. Pattern instructions page 52

Jelly beanies – a wonderfully simple hat in jelly bean colours.

Knitted in Cashsoft Baby DK, shown here in Chicory [shown with Tommy opposite] and Pixie. Pattern instructions page 62

'I'm Clarissa the cat. Aren't I purrffect with my beautiful ribbon collar?'

Knitted in Cashsoft Baby DK, shown here in Pixie. Pattern instructions page 65

'Daphne duck is my name and you'll be just quackers about how soft and cuddly I am.'

Knitted in Cashsoft Baby DK, shown here in Limone & Imp. Pattern instructions page 67

Daisies – a front buttoning cardigan with a textured moss stitch detail and lazy daisy embroidery to complete effect.

Knitted in Cashsoft Baby DK, shown here in Horseradish, Chicory, Pixie, Crocus & Cloud. Pattern instructions page 44

Sleep, baby, sleep,

Thy papa guards the sheep;

Thy mama shakes the dreamland tree

And from it fall sweet dreams for thee,

Sleep, baby, sleep,

Bunnykins – bunnies scamper all over this sweater which buttons at the back.

Knitted in Cashsoft Baby DK, shown here in Cloud & Horseradish. Pattern instructions page 42

Tension

Obtaining the correct tension is perhaps the single factor which can make the difference between a successful garment and a disastrous one. It controls both the shape and size of an article, so any variation, however slight, can distort the finished garment. Different designers feature in our books and it is **their** tension, given at the **start** of each pattern, which you must match. We recommend that you knit a square in pattern and/or stocking stitch (depending on the pattern instructions) of perhaps 5 - 10 more stitches and 5 - 10 more rows than those given in the tension note. Mark out the central 10cm square with pins. If you have too many stitches to 10cm try again using thicker needles, if you have too few stitches to 10cm try again using finer needles. Once you have achieved the correct tension your garment will be knitted to the measurements indicated in the size diagram shown at the end of the pattern.

Sizing and Size Diagram Note

The instructions are given for the smallest size. Where they vary, work the figures in brackets for the larger sizes. **One set of figures refers to all sizes.** Included with most patterns in this magazine is a '**size diagram**', or sketch of the finished garment and its dimensions. The size diagram shows the finished width of the garment at the under-arm point, and it is this measurement that the knitter should choose first; a useful tip is to measure one of your own garments which is a comfortable fit. Having chosen a size based on width, look at the corresponding length for that size; if you are not happy with the total length which we recommend, adjust your own garment before beginning your armhole shaping - any adjustment after this point will mean that your sleeve will not fit into your garment easily - don't forget to take your adjustment into account if there is any side seam shaping. Finally, look at the sleeve length; the size diagram shows the finished sleeve measurement, taking into account any top-arm insertion length. Measure your body between the centre of your neck and your wrist, this measurement should correspond to half the garment width plus the sleeve length. Again, your sleeve length may be adjusted, but remember to take into consideration your sleeve increases if you do adjust the length - you must increase more frequently than the pattern states to shorten your sleeve, less frequently to lengthen it.

Chart Note

Many of the patterns in the book are worked from charts. Each square on a chart represents a stitch and each line of squares a row of knitting. Each colour used is given a different letter and these are shown in the **materials** section, or in the **key** alongside the chart of each pattern. When working from the charts, read odd rows (K) from right to left and even rows (P) from left to right, unless otherwise stated.

Knitting with colour

There are two main methods of working colour into a knitted fabric: **Intarsia** and **Fairisle** techniques. The first method produces a single thickness of fabric and is usually used where a colour is only required in a particular area of a row and does not form a repeating pattern across the row, as in the fairisle technique.

Intarsia: The simplest way to do this is to cut short lengths of yarn for each motif or block of colour used in a row. Then joining in the various colours at the appropriate point on the row, link one colour to the next by twisting them around each other where they meet on the wrong side to avoid gaps. All ends can then either be darned along the colour join lines, as each motif is completed or then can be "knitted-in" to the fabric of the knitting as each colour is worked into the pattern. This is done in much the same way as "weaving-in" yarns when working the Fairisle technique and does save time darning-in ends. It is essential that the tension is noted for **Intarsia** as this may vary from the stocking stitch if both are used in the same pattern.

Fairisle type knitting: When two or three colours are worked repeatedly across a row, strand the yarn **not** in use loosely behind the stitches being worked. If you are working with more than two colours, treat the "floating" yarns as if they were one yarn and always spread the stitches to their correct width to keep them elastic. It is advisable not to carry the stranded or "floating" yarns over more than three stitches at a time, but to weave them under and over the colour you are working. The "floating" yarns are therefore caught at the back of the work.

Finishing Instructions

After working for hours knitting a garment, it seems a great pity that many garments are spoiled because such little care is taken in the pressing and finishing process. Follow the following tips for a truly professional-looking garment.

Pressing

Block out each piece of knitting and following the instructions on the ball band press the garment pieces, omitting the ribs. Tip: Take special care to press the edges, as this will make sewing up both easier and neater. If the ball band indicates that the fabric is not to be pressed, then covering the blocked out fabric with a damp white cotton cloth and leaving it to stand will have the desired effect. Darn in all ends neatly along the selvage edge or a colour join, as appropriate.

Stitching

When stitching the pieces together, remember to match areas of colour and texture very carefully where they meet. Use a seam stitch such as back stitch or mattress stitch for all main knitting seams and join all ribs and neckband with mattress stitch, unless otherwise stated.

Construction

Having completed the pattern instructions, join left shoulder and neckband seams as detailed above. Sew the top of the sleeve to the body of the garment using the method detailed in the pattern, referring to the appropriate guide:

Shallow set-in sleeves: Place centre of cast-off edge of sleeve to shoulder seam. Join cast-off sts at beg of next armhole shaping to cast-off sts at start of sleeve-head shaping. Sew sleeve head into armhole, easing in shapings.

Join side and sleeve seams.
Slip stitch pocket edgings and linings into place.
Sew on buttons to correspond with buttonholes.
Ribbed welts and neckbands and any area of garter stitch should not be pressed.

Abbreviations

K	knit	WS	wrong side
P	purl	psso	pass slipped
st(s)	stitch(es)		stitch over
inc	increase(e)(ing)	sl 1	slip one stitch
dec	decrease(e)(ing)	tbl	through back
st st	stocking stitch		of loop
	(1 row K, 1 row P)	M1	make one stitch
g st	garter stitch		by picking up
	(K every row)		horizontal loop
beg	begin(ning)		before next stitch
foll	following		and working into
rem	remain(ing)		back of it
rep	repeat	yrn	yarn round needle
alt	alternate	yfwd	yarn forward
cont	continue	meas	measures
patt	pattern	o	no stitches,
tog	together		times, or rows
mm	millimetres	-	no stitches, times
cm	centimetres		or rows for that
in(s)	inch(es)		size
RS	right side	approx	approximately

 = Easy, straight forward knitting    = Suitable for the average knitter   = For the more experienced knitter

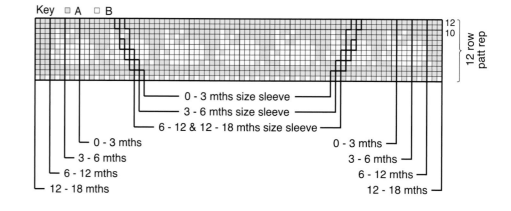

Bunnykins

YARN

	0-3	3-6	6-12	12-18 months	
To fit chest	41	46	51	56	cm
	16	18	20	22	in

RYC Cashsoft Baby DK

A Cloud	805	3	3	4	4	x 50gm
B Horseradish	801	2	2	2	3	x 50gm

NEEDLES

1 pair 3¼mm (no 10) (US 3) needles
1 pair 4mm (no 8) (US 6) needles

BUTTONS – 3 x 00401

TENSION

25 sts and 29 rows to 10 cm measured over patterned stocking stitch using 4mm (US 6) needles.

BACK

Using 3¼mm (US 3) needles and yarn A cast on 55 [61: 66: 71] sts.
Work in g st for 3 rows, ending with **WS** facing for next row.
Row 4 (WS): K3 [6: 5: 4], M1, *K7, M1, rep from * to last 3 [6: 5: 4] sts, K to end. 63 [69: 75: 81] sts.
Change to 4mm (US 6) needles.
Beg and ending rows as indicated, using the **fairisle** technique as described on the information page and repeating the 12 row patt repeat throughout, cont in patt from chart, which is worked entirely in st st beg with a K row, as folls:
Cont straight until back meas 14 [16: 18: 21] cm, ending with RS facing for next row.
Shape armholes
Keeping patt correct, cast off 3 sts at beg of next 2 rows.
57 [63: 69: 75] sts.
Dec 1 st at each end of next 3 rows.
51 [57: 63: 69] sts.**
Cont straight until armhole meas 4 [5: 6: 7] cm, ending with RS facing for next row.
Divide for back opening
Next row (RS): Patt 24 [27: 30: 33] sts and turn, leaving rem sts on a holder.
Work each side of neck separately.
Cont straight until armhole meas 11 [12: 13: 14] cm,

ending with RS facing for next row.
Shape shoulder and back neck
Cast off 6 [8: 9: 10] sts at beg of next row, then 11 [11: 12: 13] sts at beg of foll row.
Cast off rem 7 [8: 9: 10] sts.
With RS facing, rejoin yarns to rem sts, cast off centre 3 sts, patt to end.
Complete to match first side, reversing shapings.

FRONT

Work as given for back to **.
Cont straight until 6 [6: 6: 8] rows less have been worked than on back to beg of shoulder shaping, ending with RS facing for next row.
Shape neck
Next row (RS): Patt 17 [20: 22: 25] sts and turn, leaving rem sts on a holder.
Work each side of neck separately.
Dec 1 st at neck edge on next 3 rows, then on foll 1 [1: 1: 2] alt rows, ending with RS facing for next row. 13 [16: 18: 20] sts.
Shape shoulder
Cast off 6 [8: 9: 10] sts at beg of next row.
Work 1 row.
Cast off rem 7 [8: 9: 10] sts.
With RS facing, rejoin yarns to rem sts, cast off centre 17 [17: 19: 19] sts, patt to end.
Complete to match first side, reversing shapings.

SLEEVES

Using 3¼mm (US 3) needles and yarn A cast on 33 [34: 36: 36] sts.
Work in g st for 3 rows, ending with **WS** facing for

next row.
Row 4 (WS): K6 [3: 4: 4], M1, *K7, M1, rep from * to last 6 [3: 4: 4] sts, K to end. 37 [39: 41: 41] sts.
Change to 4mm (US 6) needles.
Beg and ending rows as indicated, cont in patt from chart, shaping sides by inc 1 st at each end of 3rd and foll 2 [3: 2: 1] alt rows, then on every foll 4th row until there are 57 [61: 65: 69] sts, taking inc sts into patt.
Cont straight until sleeve meas 16 [17: 20: 23] cm, ending with RS facing for next row.
Shape top
Keeping patt correct, cast off 3 sts at beg of next 2 rows. 51 [55: 59: 63] sts.
Dec 1 st at each end of next and foll 2 alt rows, then on foll row, ending with RS facing for next row.
Cast off rem 43 [47: 51: 55] sts.

MAKING UP

Press as described on the information page.
Join both shoulder seams using back stitch, or mattress stitch if preferred.
Button band
With RS facing, using 3¼mm (US 3) needles and yarn A, pick up and knit 15 sts down right back opening edge, from neck shaping to base of opening.
Work in g st for 4 rows, ending with **WS** facing for next row.
Cast off knitwise (on **WS**).
Buttonhole band
With RS facing, using 3¼mm (US 3) needles and

Key ☐ A ☐ B

0 - 3 mths size sleeve
3 - 6 mths size sleeve
6 - 12 & 12 - 18 mths size sleeve

0 - 3 mths
3 - 6 mths
6 - 12 mths
12 - 18 mths

0 - 3 mths
3 - 6 mths
6 - 12 mths
12 - 18 mths

12
10

12 row patt rep

yarn A, pick up and knit 15 sts up left back opening edge, from base of opening to neck shaping.

Row 1 (WS): Knit.

Row 2: K3, (K2tog, yfwd, K4) twice.

Work in g st for a further 2 rows, ending with **WS** facing for next row.

Cast off knitwise (on **WS**).

Neckband

With RS facing, using 3¼mm (US 3) needles and yarn A, beg and ending at cast-off edges of back bands, pick up and knit 14 [14: 15: 16] sts from left back, 8 [8: 8: 10] sts down left side of neck, 17 [17: 19: 19] sts from front, 8 [8: 8: 10] sts up right side of neck, then 14 [14: 15: 16] sts from right back. 61 [61: 65: 71] sts.

Row 1 (WS): Knit.

Row 2: K1, K2tog, yfwd, K to end.

Work in g st for a further 2 rows, ending with **WS** facing for next row.

Cast off knitwise (on **WS**).

See information page for finishing instructions, setting in sleeves using the shallow set-in method.

25 [27.5: 30: 32.5] cm
(10 [11: 12: 13] in)

25 [28: 31: 35] cm
(10 [11: 12: 14] in)

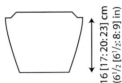

16 [17: 20: 23] cm
(6½ [6½: 8: 9] in)

 Daisies

YARN

	0-3	3-6	6-12	12-18	months
To fit chest	41	46	51	56	cm
	16	18	20	22	in

RYC Cashsoft Baby DK

	3	3	4	5	x 50gm

Oddments of same yarn in 4 contrast colours
for embroidery
(photographed in Horseradish 801, with
embroidery in Chicory 804, Pixie 807, Crocus 808
and Cloud 805)

NEEDLES

1 pair 3¼mm (no 10) (US 3) needles
1 pair 4mm (no 8) (US 6) needles

BUTTONS – 6 x 00318

TENSION

22 sts and 30 rows to 10 cm measured over
stocking stitch using 4mm (US 6) needles.

BACK

Using 3¼mm (US 3) needles cast on 55 [61:
67: 73] sts.
Row 1 (RS): K1, *P1, K1, rep from * to end.
Row 2: As row 1.
These 2 rows form moss st.
Work in moss st for a further 8 rows, ending with
RS facing for next row.
Change to 4mm (US 6) needles.
Row 1 (RS): K4 [5: 6: 7], moss st 3 sts, K9 [10:
11: 12], moss st 3 sts, K17 [19: 21: 23], moss st
3 sts, K9 [10: 11: 12], moss st 3 sts, K to end.
Row 2: P4 [5: 6: 7], moss st 3 sts, P9 [10: 11: 12],
moss st 3 sts, P17 [19: 21: 23], moss st 3 sts,
P9 [10: 11: 12], moss st 3 sts, P to end.
These 2 rows set the sts.
Cont as set until back meas 14 [16: 18: 21] cm,
ending with RS facing for next row.
Beg with a K row, cont in st st as folls:
Shape armholes
Cast off 3 sts at beg of next 2 rows.
49 [55: 61: 67] sts.
Dec 1 st at each end of next 3 rows.
43 [49: 55: 61] sts.
Cont straight until armhole meas 11 [12: 13: 14] cm,
ending with RS facing for next row.

Shape shoulders and back neck
Next row (RS): Cast off 5 [6: 7: 8] sts, K until
there are 6 [8: 9: 10] sts on right needle and turn,
leaving rem sts on a holder.
Work each side of neck separately.
Dec 1 st at neck edge on next row.
Cast off rem 5 [7: 8: 9] sts.
With RS facing, rejoin yarn to rem sts, cast off
centre 21 [21: 23: 25] sts, K to end.
Complete to match first side, reversing shapings.

LEFT FRONT
Using 3¼mm (US 3) needles cast on 35 [38:
41: 44] sts.
Row 1 (RS): *K1, P1, rep from * to last 1 [0: 1: 0]
st, K1 [0: 1: 0].
Row 2: K1 [0: 1: 0], *P1, K1, rep from * to end.
These 2 rows form moss st.
Work in moss st for a further 7 rows, ending with
WS facing for next row.
Row 10 (WS): Moss st 7 sts and slip these sts
onto a holder, moss st to end. 28 [31: 34: 37] sts.
Change to 4mm (US 6) needles.
Row 1 (RS): K4 [5: 6: 7], moss st 3 sts, K9 [10:
11: 12], moss st 3 sts, K to end.
Row 2: (P9 [10: 11: 12], moss st 3 sts) twice,
P to end.
These 2 rows set the sts.
Cont as set until left front matches back to beg
of armhole shaping, ending with RS facing for
next row.
Beg with a K row, cont in st st as folls:
Shape armhole
Cast off 3 sts at beg of next row.
25 [28: 31: 34] sts.
Work 1 row.
Dec 1 st at armhole edge of next 3 rows.
22 [25: 28: 31] sts.
Cont straight until 7 [7: 7: 9] rows less have been
worked than on back to beg of shoulder shaping,
ending with **WS** facing for next row.
Shape neck
Cast off 7 [7: 8: 8] sts at beg of next row.
15 [18: 20: 23] sts.
Dec 1 st at neck edge on next 4 rows, then on
foll 1 [1: 1: 2] alt rows, ending with RS facing for
next row.
10 [13: 15: 17] sts.

Shape shoulder
Cast off 5 [6: 7: 8] sts at beg of next row.
Work 1 row.
Cast off rem 5 [7: 8: 9] sts.

RIGHT FRONT
Using 3¼mm (US 3) needles cast on 35 [38:
41: 44] sts.
Row 1 (RS): K1 [0: 1: 0], *P1, K1, rep from * to end.
Row 2: *K1, P1, rep from * to last 1 [0: 1: 0] st,
K1 [0: 1: 0].
These 2 rows form moss st.
Work in moss st for a further 2 rows, ending with
RS facing for next row.
Row 5 (RS): Moss st 2 sts, work 2 tog,
yrn (to make a buttonhole), moss st to end.
Work in moss st for a further 4 rows, ending with
WS facing for next row.
Row 10 (WS): Moss st to last 7 sts and turn,
leaving rem 7 sts on a holder. 28 [31: 34: 37] sts.
Change to 4mm (US 6) needles.
Row 1 (RS): (K9 [10: 11: 12], moss st 3 sts) twice,
K to end.
Row 2: P4 [5: 6: 7], moss st 3 sts, P9 [10: 11: 12],
moss st 3 sts, P to end.
These 2 rows set the sts.
Complete to match left front, reversing shapings.

SLEEVES
Using 3¼mm (US 3) needles cast on 33 [35:
37: 39] sts.
Work in moss st as given for back for 10 rows,
ending with RS facing for next row.
Change to 4mm (US 6) needles.
Beg with a K row, cont in st st, shaping sides by
inc 1 st at each end of next and every foll alt [alt:
alt: 4th] row to 37 [41: 41: 59] sts, then on every
foll 4th [4th: 4th: 6th] row until there are 51 [55:
59: 63] sts.
Cont straight until sleeve meas 16 [17: 20: 23] cm,
ending with RS facing for next row.
Shape top
Cast off 3 sts at beg of next 2 rows.
45 [49: 53: 57] sts.
Dec 1 st at each end of next and foll 2 alt rows,
then on foll row, ending with RS facing for next
row.
Cast off rem 37 [41: 45: 49] sts.

MAKING UP

Press as described on the information page.
Join both shoulder seams using back stitch, or
mattress stitch if preferred.

Button band

Slip 7 sts from left front holder onto 3¼mm (US 3)
needles and rejoin yarn with RS facing.
Cont in moss st as set until button band, when
slightly stretched, fits up left front opening edge
to neck shaping, ending with RS facing for next
row.
Break yarn and leave sts on a holder.
Slip stitch band in place.
Mark positions for 6 buttons on this band – first
to come level with buttonhole already worked in
right front, last to come just above neck shaping,
and rem 4 buttons evenly spaced between.

Buttonhole band

Slip 7 sts from right front holder onto 3¼mm
(US 3) needles and rejoin yarn with **WS** facing.
Cont in moss st as set until buttonhole band,
when slightly stretched, fits up right front
opening edge to neck shaping, ending with RS
facing for next row and with the addition of a
further 4 buttonholes worked to correspond with
positions marked for buttons as folls:
Buttonhole row (RS): Moss st 2 sts, work 2 tog,
yrn (to make a buttonhole), moss st 3 sts.
When band is complete, do NOT break yarn.
Slip stitch band in place.

Neckband

With RS facing and using 3¼mm (US 3) needles,
moss st 7 sts of buttonhole band, pick up and
knit 15 [15: 16: 18] sts up right side of neck,
25 [25: 27: 29] sts from back, and 15 [15: 16: 18]
sts down left side of neck, then moss st 7 sts of
button band. 69 [69: 73: 79] sts.
Work in moss st as set by bands for 1 row, ending
with RS facing for next row.
Row 2 (RS): Moss st 2 sts, work 2 tog,
yrn (to make 6th buttonhole), moss st to end.
Work in moss st for a further 4 rows, ending with
WS facing for next row.
Cast off in moss st (on **WS**).
See information page for finishing instructions,
setting in sleeves using the shallow set-in method.

Embroidery

Using photograph as a guide, embroider daisies
onto fronts. For each daisy, work 8 lazy daisy sts
radiating out from one point using first colour.
Using second colour, embroider a bullion knot at
centre and at end of each petal.

25 [27.5: 30.5: 33] cm
(10 [11: 12: 13] in)

25 [28: 31: 35] cm
(10 [11: 12: 14] in)

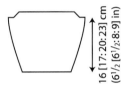

16 [17: 20: 23] cm
(6½ [6½: 8: 9] in)

Lazy Daisy

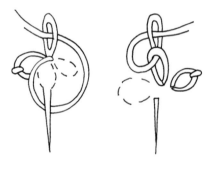

Bullion Knot

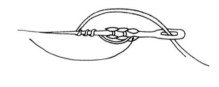

Bobby

YARN

	0-3	3-6	6-12	12-18 months	
To fit chest	41	46	51	56	cm
	16	18	20	22	in

RYC Cashsoft Baby DK

A Crocus	808	2	2	2	3	x 50gm
B Horseradish	801	2	2	2	2	x 50gm
C Cloud	805	2	2	2	2	x 50gm

NEEDLES

1 pair 3¼mm (no 10) (US 3) needles
1 pair 4mm (no 8) (US 6) needles

BUTTONS – 5 x 00394

TENSION

22 sts and 30 rows to 10 cm measured over stocking stitch using 4mm (US 6) needles.

BACK

Using 3¼mm (US 3) needles and yarn A cast on 57 [63: 69: 75] sts.
Work in g st for 6 rows, ending with RS facing for next row.
Change to 4mm (US 6) needles.
Joining in colours as required and beg with a K row, cont in striped st st as folls:
Using yarn B, work 2 rows.
Using yarn C, work 2 rows.
Using yarn A, work 2 rows.
These 6 rows form striped st st.
Cont in striped st st until back meas 14 [16: 18: 21] cm, ending with RS facing for next row.
Shape raglan armholes
Keeping stripes correct, cast off 3 sts at beg of next 2 rows. 51 [57: 63: 69] sts.
0-3 months only
Dec 1 st at each end of next and foll 4th row. 47 sts.
Work 3 rows.
All sizes
Dec 1 st at each end of next 1 [1: 3: 5] rows, then on every foll alt row until 21 [21: 23: 25] sts rem.
Work 1 row, ending with RS facing for next row.
Cast off.

LEFT FRONT

Using 3¼mm (US 3) needles and yarn A cast on 34 [37: 40: 43] sts.

For a girl
Work in g st for 5 rows, ending with **WS** facing for next row.
For a boy
Work in g st for 4 rows, ending with RS facing for next row.
Row 5 (RS): K to last 3 sts, yfwd, K2tog, K1.
For a girl or a boy
Row 6 (WS): K5 and slip these sts onto a holder, K to end.
29 [32: 35: 38] sts.
Change to 4mm (US 6) needles.
Beg with a K row and 2 rows using yarn B, cont in striped st st as given for back until left front matches back to beg of raglan armhole shaping, ending with RS facing for next row.
Shape raglan armhole
Keeping stripes correct, cast off 3 sts at beg of next row.
26 [29: 32: 35] sts.
Work 1 row.
0-3 months only
Dec 1 st at raglan armhole edge of next and foll 4th row. 24 sts.
Work 3 rows.
All sizes
Dec 1 st at raglan armhole edge of next 1 [1: 3: 5] rows, then on every foll alt row until 15 [15: 16: 18] sts rem, ending with **WS** facing for next row.
Shape neck
Keeping stripes correct, cast off 10 [10: 11: 11] sts at beg of next row. 5 [5: 5: 7] sts.
Dec 1 st at neck edge on next 2 [2: 2: 3] rows **and at same time** dec 1 st at raglan armhole edge on next and foll 0 [0: 0: 1] alt row. 2 sts.
Work 0 [0: 0: 1] row.
Next row (RS): K2tog and fasten off.

RIGHT FRONT

Using 3¼mm (US 3) needles and yarn A cast on 34 [37: 40: 43] sts.
For a girl
Work in g st for 4 rows, ending with RS facing for next row.
Row 5 (RS): K1, K2tog, yfwd, K to end.
For a boy
Work in g st for 5 rows, ending with **WS** facing for next row.

For a girl or a boy
Row 6 (WS): K to last 5 sts and turn, leaving rem 5 sts on a holder. 29 [32: 35: 38] sts.
Change to 4mm (US 6) needles and complete to match left front, reversing shapings.

SLEEVES

Using 3¼mm (US 3) needles and yarn A cast on 37 [39: 41: 43] sts.
Work in g st for 6 rows, ending with RS facing for next row.
Change to 4mm (US 6) needles.
Beg with a K row and 2 rows using yarn A, cont in striped st st as given for back, shaping sides by inc 1 st at each end of 3rd and every foll 4th [4th: 6th: 8th] row to 43 [43: 53: 59] sts, then on every foll 6th [6th: 8th: -] row until there are 53 [55: 57: -] sts.
Cont straight until sleeve meas approx 18 [19: 22: 25] cm, ending after same stripe row as on back to beg of raglan armhole shaping and with RS facing for next row.
Shape raglan
Keeping stripes correct, cast off 3 sts at beg of next 2 rows. 47 [49: 51: 53] sts.
Dec 1 st at each end of next and every foll alt row until 19 sts rem.
Work 1 row, ending with RS facing for next row.
Left sleeve only
Dec 1 st at each end of next row, then cast off 3 sts at beg of foll row. 14 sts.
Dec 1 st at beg of next row, then cast off 4 sts at beg of foll row. 9 sts.
Rep last 2 rows once more.
Right sleeve only
Cast off 4 sts at beg and dec 1 st at end of next row. 14 sts.
Work 1 row.
Rep last 2 rows twice more.
Both sleeves
Cast off rem 4 sts.

MAKING UP

Press as described on the information page.
Join raglan seams using back stitch, or mattress stitch if preferred.
Hood
With RS facing, using 4mm (US 6) needles and

yarn A, beg and ending at front opening edges, pick up and knit 14 [14: 15: 17] sts up right side of neck, 12 sts from right sleeve, 21 [21: 23: 25] sts from back, 12 sts from left sleeve, then 14 [14: 15: 17] sts down left side of neck.

73 [73: 77: 83] sts.

Beg with a P row and a further 1 row using yarn A, cont in striped st st as given for back as folls:

Place marker on centre st of last row.

Work 3 rows, ending with RS facing for next row.

Next row (RS): K to marked st, M1, K marked st, M1, K to end.

Rep last 4 rows 3 times more. 81 [81: 85: 91] sts.

Cont straight until hood meas 20 [21: 22: 23] cm from pick-up row, ending with RS facing for next row.

Next row (RS): K to within 2 sts of marked st, K2tog tbl, K marked st, K2tog, K to end.

Work 1 row.

Rep last 2 rows once more, then first of these rows (the dec row) again. 75 [75: 79: 85] sts.

Next row (WS): P to within 1 st of marked st, P2tog, P to end.

74 [74: 78: 84] sts.

Next row: K37 [37: 39: 42] and turn.

Fold hood in half with RS facing and, using a spare 4mm (US 6) needle, cast off both sets of sts together, taking one st from first needle tog with corresponding st from second needle.

Mark positions for 5 buttons along one front opening edge (left front for a girl, or right front for a boy) – first to come level with buttonhole already worked in front, last to come 3 cm below

neck shaping, and rem 3 buttons evenly spaced between.

Left front band

Slip 5 sts from left front holder onto 3¼mm (US 3) needles and rejoin yarn A with RS facing.

For a girl

Cont in g st until left front band, when slightly stretched, fits up entire left front opening edge to seam at top of hood, ending with RS facing for next row.

For a boy

Cont in g st until left front band, when slightly stretched, fits up entire left front opening edge to seam at top of hood, ending with RS facing for next row and with the addition of a further 4 buttonholes worked to correspond with positions marked for buttons as folls:

Buttonhole row (RS): K2, yfwd, K2tog, K1.

For a girl or a boy

Cast off.

Slip stitch band in place.

Right front band

Slip 5 sts from right front holder onto 3¼mm (US 3) needles and rejoin yarn A with **WS** facing.

For a girl

Cont in g st until right front band, when slightly stretched, fits up entire right front opening edge to seam at top of hood, ending with RS facing for next row and with the addition of a further 4 buttonholes worked to correspond with positions marked for buttons as folls:

Buttonhole row (RS): K1, K2tog, yfwd, K2.

For a boy

Cont in g st until right front band, when slightly stretched, fits up entire right front opening edge to seam at top of hood, ending with RS facing for next row.

For a girl or a boy

Cast off.

Slip stitch band in place, joining cast-off edges at hood seam.

See information page for finishing instructions.

26 [29: 31: 35] cm
(10 [11½: 12: 14] in)

26 [28.5: 31.5: 34] cm
(10 [11: 12½: 13½] in)

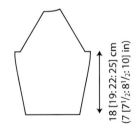

18 [19: 22: 25] cm
(7 [7½: 8½: 10] in)

Tommy

YARN

	0-3	3-6	6-12	12-18	months
To fit chest	41	46	51	56	cm
	16	18	20	22	in
RYC Cashcotton DK					
	2	2	3	3	x 50gm

(photographed in Wheat 615)

NEEDLES

1 pair 3¼mm (no 10) (US 3) needles
1 pair 4mm (no 8) (US 6) needles
Cable needle

BUTTONS – 2 x 00321

TENSION

22 sts and 30 rows to 10 cm measured over stocking stitch using 4mm (US 6) needles.

SPECIAL ABBREVIATIONS

C8B = slip next 4 sts onto cable needle and leave at back of work, K4, then K4 from cable needle.

BACK

Using 3¼mm (US 3) needles cast on 51 [57: 63: 69] sts.
Row 1 (RS): P3, *K3, P3, rep from * to end.
Row 2: K3, *P3, K3, rep from * to end.
These 2 rows form rib.
Cont in rib for a further 7 rows, ending with **WS** facing for next row.
Row 10 (WS): Rib 9 [10: 11: 12], (M1, rib 2, M1, rib 3, M1, rib 9 [11: 13: 15]) twice, M1, rib 2, M1, rib 3, M1, rib to end. 60 [66: 72: 78] sts.
Change to 4mm (US 6) needles.
Row 1 (RS): K0 [1: 0: 1], (P1, K1) 4 [4: 5: 5] times, *P1, K8, P1, (K1, P1) 3 [4: 5: 6] times, K1, rep from * once more, P1, K8, P1, (K1, P1) 4 [4: 5: 5] times, K0 [1: 0: 1].

Row 2: K0 [1: 0: 1], (P1, K1) 4 [4: 5: 5] times, *K1, P8, K1, (K1, P1) 3 [4: 5: 6] times, K1, rep from * once more, K1, P8, K1, (K1, P1) 4 [4: 5: 5] times, K0 [1: 0: 1].
Row 3: K0 [1: 0: 1], (P1, K1) 4 [4: 5: 5] times, *P1, C8B, P1, (K1, P1) 3 [4: 5: 6] times, K1, rep from * once more, P1, C8B, P1, (K1, P1) 4 [4: 5: 5] times, K0 [1: 0: 1].
Row 4: As row 2.
Rows 5 to 10: As rows 1 and 2, 3 times.
These 10 rows form patt.
Cont in patt until back meas 13 [15: 17: 20] cm, ending with RS facing for next row.
Shape armholes
Keeping patt correct, cast off 4 sts at beg of next 2 rows. 52 [58: 64: 70] sts.
Dec 1 st at each end of next 3 rows, then on foll 0 [1: 2: 3] alt rows.
46 [50: 54: 58] sts.
Cont straight until armhole meas 11 [12: 13: 14] cm, ending with RS facing for next row.
Shape shoulders and back neck
Next row (RS): Cast off 5 [6: 6: 7] sts, patt until there are 6 [7: 8: 8] sts on right needle and turn, leaving rem sts on a holder.
Work each side of neck separately.
Dec 1 st at neck edge on next row.
Cast off rem 5 [6: 7: 7] sts.
With RS facing, rejoin yarn to rem sts, cast off centre 24 [24: 26: 28] sts, patt to end.
Complete to match first side, reversing shapings.

FRONT

Work as given for back until 8 [8: 8: 10] rows less have been worked than on back to beg of shoulder shaping, ending with RS facing for next row.
Shape neck
Next row (RS): Patt 13 [15: 16: 18] sts and turn, leaving rem sts on a holder.

Work each side of neck separately.
Dec 1 st at neck edge on next 3 rows, then on foll 0 [0: 0: 1] alt row, ending with RS facing for next row. 10 [12: 13: 14] sts.
Shape shoulder
Cast off 5 [6: 6: 7] sts at beg of next row.
Work 1 row.
Cast off rem 5 [6: 7: 7] sts.
With RS facing, rejoin yarn to rem sts, cast off centre 20 [20: 22: 22] sts, patt to end.
Dec 1 st at neck edge on next 3 rows, then on foll 0 [0: 0: 1] alt row.
10 [12: 13: 14] sts.
Work 5 rows, ending with **WS** facing for next row.
Shape shoulder
Cast off 5 [6: 6: 7] sts at beg of next row.
Work 1 row.
Cast off rem 5 [6: 7: 7] sts.

MAKING UP

Press as described on the information page.
Join right shoulder seam using back stitch, or mattress stitch if preferred.
Neckband
With RS facing and using 3¼mm (US 3) needles, pick up and knit 4 [4: 4: 6] sts down left side of neck, 18 [18: 21: 21] sts from front, 8 [8: 8: 10] sts up right side of neck, then 23 [23: 26: 28] sts from back. 53 [53: 59: 65] sts.
Row 1 (WS): K1, P3, *K3, P3, rep from * to last st, K1.
Row 2: K4, *P3, K3, rep from * to last st, K1.
These 2 rows form rib.
Work in rib for a further 2 rows, ending with **WS** facing for next row.
Cast off in rib (on **WS**).
Back shoulder button band
With RS facing and using 3¼mm (US 3) needles, pick up and knit 15 sts across left back shoulder

edge, from top of neckband to armhole edge.
Beg with row 2, work in rib as given for back for
4 rows, ending with **WS** facing for next row.
Cast off in rib (on **WS**).

Front shoulder buttonhole band
With RS facing and using 3¼mm (US 3) needles,
pick up and knit 15 sts across left front shoulder
edge, from armhole edge to top of neckband.
Beg with row 2, work in rib as given for back for
1 row, ending with RS facing for next row.
Row 2 (RS): Rib 3, work 2 tog, yrn (to make first
buttonhole), rib 6, work 2 tog, yrn (to make
second buttonhole), rib 2.
Work in rib for a further 2 rows, ending with **WS**
facing for next row.
Cast off in rib (on **WS**).
Lay front shoulder buttonhole band over back
shoulder button band so that pick-up rows match
cast-off edges and sew together at armhole edge.

Armhole borders (both alike)
With RS facing and using 3¼mm (US 3) needles,
pick up and knit 51 [57: 63: 69] sts evenly all
round armhole edge.
Beg with row 2, work in rib as given for back for
4 rows, ending with **WS** facing for next row.
Cast off in rib (on **WS**).
See information page for finishing instructions.

24 [27: 30: 34] cm
(9½ [10½: 12: 13½] in)

23 [26: 28.5: 31.5] cm
(9 [10: 11: 12½] in)

🧶🧶 ⋮ **Stripy**

YARN

	1-2	2-3	3-4	4-5	years
To fit chest	56	58	61	64	cm
	22	23	24	25	in

RYC Cashsoft Baby DK

A Blue Boy	809	2	2	2	3	x 50gm
B Horseradish	801	2	2	2	3	x 50gm
C Cloud	805	1	1	2	2	x 50gm

NEEDLES

1 pair 3¼mm (no 10) (US 3) needles
1 pair 4mm (no 8) (US 6) needles

BUTTONS – 2 x 00392

TENSION

22 sts and 30 rows to 10 cm measured over stocking stitch using 4mm (US 6) needles.

STRIPE SEQUENCE

Beg with a K row, work in st st using colours as folls:
Rows 1 and 2: Using yarn B.
Rows 3 and 4: Using yarn A.
Rows 5 and 6: Using yarn B.
Rows 7 and 8: Using yarn C.
Rows 9 to 16: Using yarn B.
Rows 17 to 24: Using yarn A.
Rows 25 to 32: Using yarn B.
Rows 33 to 40: Using yarn C.
These 40 rows form stripe sequence and are repeated as required.

BACK

Using 3¼mm (US 3) needles and yarn A cast on 66 [70: 74: 78] sts.
Row 1 (RS): K2, *P2, K2, rep from * to end.
Row 2: P2, *K2, P2, rep from * to end.
These 2 rows form rib.
Cont in rib for a further 8 rows, inc 1 st at each end of last row and ending with RS facing for next row.
68 [72: 76: 80] sts.
Change to 4mm (US 6) needles.
Joining in and breaking off colours as required

and beg with a K row, cont in st st in stripe sequence as folls:
Cont straight until back meas 17 [18: 20: 21] cm, ending with RS facing for next row.
Shape armholes
Keeping stripes correct, cast off 4 sts at beg of next 2 rows. 60 [64: 68: 72] sts.
Dec 1 st at each end of next 3 rows.
54 [58: 62: 66] sts.
Cont straight until armhole meas 14 [15: 15: 16] cm, ending with RS facing for next row.
Shape shoulders and back neck
Next row (RS): Cast off 7 [8: 8: 9] sts, K until there are 9 [9: 10: 10] sts on right needle and turn, leaving rem sts on a holder.
Work each side of neck separately.
Dec 1 st at neck edge on next row.
Cast off rem 8 [8: 9: 9] sts.
With RS facing, rejoin yarns to rem sts, cast off centre 22 [24: 26: 28] sts, K to end.
Complete to match first side, reversing shapings.

FRONT

Work as given for back until 26 rows less have been worked than on back to beg of shoulder shaping, ending with RS facing for next row.
Divide for front opening
Next row (RS): K24 [26: 28: 30] and turn, leaving rem sts on a holder.
Work each side of neck separately.
Work 16 rows, ending with **WS** facing for next row.
Shape neck
Keeping stripes correct, cast off 4 [5: 6: 7] sts at beg of next row. 20 [21: 22: 23] sts.
Dec 1 st at neck edge on next 5 rows.
15 [16: 17: 18] sts.
Work 3 rows, ending with RS facing for next row.
Shape shoulder
Cast off 7 [8: 8: 9] sts at beg of next row.
Work 1 row.
Cast off rem 8 [8: 9: 9] sts.
With RS facing, rejoin yarn to rem sts, cast off centre 6 sts, K to end.
Complete to match first side, reversing shapings.

SLEEVES

Using 3¼mm (US 3) needles and yarn A cast on 34 [38: 38: 42] sts.
Work in rib as given for back for 10 rows, dec 0 [1: 0: 1] st at end of last row and ending with RS facing for next row. 34 [36: 38: 40] sts.
Change to 4mm (US 6) needles.
Beg with a K row and stripe sequence row 1, cont in st st in stripe sequence, shaping sides by inc 1 st at each end of 3rd and foll 6 [5: 2: 0] alt rows, then on every foll 4th row until there are 62 [66: 66: 70] sts.
Cont straight until sleeve meas 20 [22: 24: 27] cm, ending with RS facing for next row.
Shape top
Cast off 4 sts at beg of next 2 rows.
54 [58: 58: 62] sts.
Dec 1 st at each end of next and foll 2 alt rows, then on foll row, ending with RS facing for next row.
Cast off rem 46 [50: 50: 54] sts.

MAKING UP

Press as described on the information page.
Join both shoulder seams using back stitch, or mattress stitch if preferred.
Button band
With RS facing, using 3¼mm (US 3) needles and yarn A, pick up and knit 12 sts along one side of front opening (left front for a girl, or right front for a boy), between neck shaping and base of opening.
Row 1 (WS): K1, *P2, K2, rep from * to last 3 sts, P2, K1.
Row 2: K3, *P2, K2, rep from * to last st, K1.
These 2 rows form rib.
Cont in rib for a further 5 rows, ending with RS facing for next row.
Cast off in rib.
Buttonhole band
Work to match button band, picking up sts along other side of front opening and with the addition of 2 buttonholes in row 4 as folls:
Row 4 (RS): Rib 1, work 2 tog, yrn (to make first buttonhole), rib 6, yrn (to make second buttonhole), work 2 tog, rib 1.

Collar

With RS facing, using 3¼mm (US 3) needles and yarn A, beg and ending halfway across top of bands, pick up and knit 19 [20: 21: 22] sts up right side of neck, 26 [28: 30: 32] sts from back, then 19 [20: 21: 22] sts down left side of neck. 64 [68: 72: 76] sts.

Beg with row 2, work in rib as given for button band for 17 rows, ending with RS of body (**WS** of collar) facing for next row.

Next row: K1, *P2, K1, M1, K1, rep from * to last 3 sts, P2, K1. 79 [84: 89: 94] sts.

Next row: K3, *P3, K2, rep from * to last st, K1.

Next row: K1, *P2, K3, rep from * to last 3 sts, P2, K1.

Rep last 2 rows until collar meas 9 cm from pick-up row.

Cast off in rib.

See information page for finishing instructions, setting in sleeves using the shallow set-in method.

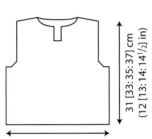

31 [32.5: 34.5: 36.5] cm
(12 [13: 13½: 14½] in)

31 [33: 35: 37] cm
(12 [13: 14: 14½] in)

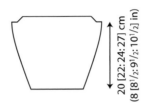

20 [22: 24: 27] cm
(8 [8½: 9½: 10½] in)

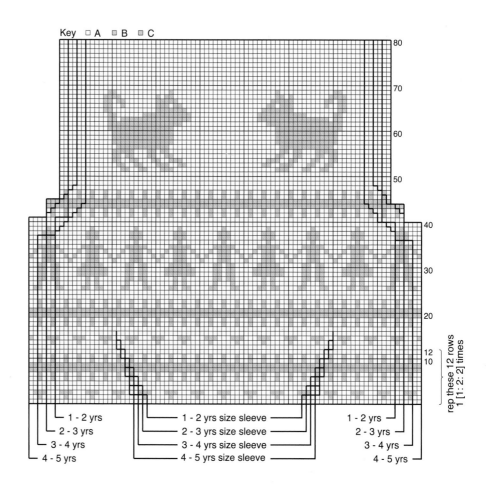

Bow-wow

YARN

	1-2	2-3	3-4	4-5	years
To fit chest	56	58	61	64	cm
	22	23	24	25	in

RYC Cashsoft Baby DK

A Horseradish	801	3	3	4	4	x 50gm
B Crocus	808	1	1	2	2	x 50gm
C Blue Boy	809	1	1	1	2	x 50gm

NEEDLES

1 pair 3¼mm (no 10) (US 3) needles
1 pair 4mm (no 8) (US 6) needles

BUTTONS – 3 x 00322

TENSION

25 sts and 29 rows to 10 cm measured over patterned stocking stitch using 4mm (US 6) needles.

BACK

Using 3¼mm (US 3) needles and yarn A cast on 70 [74: 74: 78] sts.
Row 1 (RS): K2, *P2, K2, rep from * to end.
Row 2: P2, *K2, P2, rep from * to end.
These 2 rows form rib.
Cont in rib for a further 7 rows, ending with **WS** facing for next row.
Row 10 (WS): Rib 5 [7: 2: 4], M1, *rib 10 [10: 7: 7], M1, rep from * to last 5 [7: 2: 4] sts, rib to end.
77 [81: 85: 89] sts.
Change to 4mm (US 6) needles.
Beg and ending rows as indicated and using the **fairisle** technique for rows 1 to 47 and the **intarsia** technique for rows 51 onwards, both as described on the information page, **working chart rows 1 to 12 once [once: twice: twice]** and then working chart rows 13 onwards, cont in patt from chart, which is worked entirely in st st beg with a K row, as folls:
Work 40 [44: 48: 52] rows, ending after chart row 40 [44: 36: 40] and ending with RS facing for next row. (Back should meas 17 [18: 20: 21] cm.)
Shape armholes
Keeping chart correct, cast off 4 sts at beg of next 2 rows. 69 [73: 77: 81] sts.
Dec 1 st at each end of next 3 rows.
63 [67: 71: 75] sts.**

Cont straight until armhole meas 6 [7: 7: 8] cm, ending with RS facing for next row.
Divide for back opening
Next row (RS): Patt 30 [32: 34: 36] sts and turn, leaving rem sts on a holder.
Work each side of neck separately.
Working rem rows of chart and then completing back in st st using yarn A only, cont as folls:
Cont straight until armhole meas 14 [15: 15: 16] cm, ending with RS facing for next row.
Shape shoulder and back neck
Cast off 9 [9: 10: 10] sts at beg of next row, then 12 [13: 14: 15] sts at beg of foll row.
Cast off rem 9 [10: 10: 11] sts.
With RS facing, rejoin yarn to rem sts, cast off centre 3 sts, patt to end.
Complete to match first side, reversing shapings.

FRONT

Work as given for back to **.
Working rem rows of chart and then completing front in st st using yarn A only, cont as folls:
Cont straight until 8 rows less have been worked than on back to beg of shoulder shaping, ending with RS facing for next row.
Shape neck
Next row (RS): Patt 23 [24: 25: 26] sts and turn, leaving rem sts on a holder.
Work each side of neck separately.
Dec 1 st at neck edge on next 4 rows, then on foll alt row. 18 [19: 20: 21] sts.
Work 1 row, ending with RS facing for next row.
Shape shoulder
Cast off 9 [9: 10: 10] sts at beg of next row.
Work 1 row.

Key ☐ A ▨ B ▨ C

1 - 2 yrs
2 - 3 yrs
3 - 4 yrs
4 - 5 yrs

1 - 2 yrs size sleeve
2 - 3 yrs size sleeve
3 - 4 yrs size sleeve
4 - 5 yrs size sleeve

1 - 2 yrs
2 - 3 yrs
3 - 4 yrs
4 - 5 yrs

rep these 12 rows
1 [1: 2: 2] times

Cast off rem 9 [10: 10: 11] sts.

With RS facing, rejoin yarn to rem sts, cast off centre 17 [19: 21: 23] sts, patt to end.

Complete to match first side, reversing shapings.

SLEEVES

Using 3¼mm (US 3) needles and yarn A cast on 34 [38: 38: 42] sts.

Work in rib as given for back for 10 rows, inc [dec: inc: dec] 1 st at end of last row and ending with RS facing for next row. 35 [37: 39: 41] sts.

Change to 4mm (US 6) needles.

Beg and ending rows as indicated and using the **fairisle** technique as described on the information page, work in patt from chart as folls:

Inc 1 st at each end of 3rd and foll 6 [5: 2: 0] alt rows, then on every foll 0 [0: 4th: 4th] row until there are 49 [49: 49: 49] sts, taking inc sts into patt.

Work 1 [3: 1: 1] rows, completing chart row 16 and ending with RS facing for next row.

Break off contrasts and cont using yarn A only.

Beg with a K row, cont in st st, shaping sides by inc 1 st at each end of 3rd [next: 3rd: 3rd] and every foll 4th row until there are 63 [67: 67: 71] sts.

Cont straight until sleeve meas 20 [22: 24: 27] cm, ending with RS facing for next row.

Shape top

Cast off 4 sts at beg of next 2 rows.

55 [59: 59: 63] sts.

Dec 1 st at each end of next and foll 2 alt rows, then on foll row, ending with RS facing for next row.

Cast off rem 47 [51: 51: 55] sts.

MAKING UP

Press as described on the information page.

Join both shoulder seams using back stitch, or mattress stitch if preferred.

Button band

With RS facing, using 3¼mm (US 3) needles and yarn A, pick up and knit 18 sts down right back opening edge, from neck shaping to base of opening.

Work in g st for 4 rows, ending with **WS** facing for next row.

Cast off knitwise (on **WS**).

Buttonhole band

With RS facing, using 3¼mm (US 3) needles and yarn A, pick up and knit 18 sts up left back opening edge, from base of opening to neck shaping.

Row 1 (WS): Knit.

Row 2: (K5, K2tog, yfwd) twice, K4.

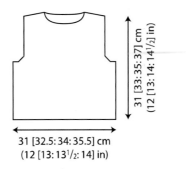

31 [32.5: 34: 35.5] cm
(12 [13: 13½: 14] in)

Work in g st for a further 2 rows, ending with **WS** facing for next row.

Cast off knitwise (on **WS**).

Neckband

With RS facing, using 3¼mm (US 3) needles and yarn A, beg and ending at cast-off edges of back bands, pick up and knit 15 [16: 17: 18] sts from left back, 9 sts down left side of neck, 17 [19: 21: 23] sts from front, 9 sts up right side of neck, then 15 [16: 17: 18] sts from right back.

65 [69: 73: 77] sts.

Row 1 (WS): Knit.

Row 2: K1, K2tog, yfwd, K to end.

Work in g st for a further 2 rows, ending with **WS** facing for next row.

Cast off knitwise (on **WS**).

See information page for finishing instructions, setting in sleeves using the shallow set-in method.

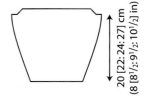

Boatman

YARN

	1-2	2-3	3-4	4-5	years
To fit chest	56	58	61	64	cm
	22	23	24	25	in

RYC Cashsoft Baby DK

A Cloud	805	2	2	2	3	x 50gm
B Blue Boy	809	2	2	2	2	x 50gm
C Horseradish	801	1	1	1	1	x 50gm
D Limone	802	1	1	1	1	x 50gm

NEEDLES

1 pair 3¼mm (no 10) (US 3) needles
1 pair 4mm (no 8) (US 6) needles
3¼mm (no 10) (US 3) circular needle

TENSION

25 sts and 29 rows to 10 cm measured over patterned stocking stitch using 4mm (US 6) needles.

BACK

Using 3¼mm (US 3) needles and yarn A cast on 58 [62: 66: 70] sts.
Row 1 (RS): K2, *P2, K2, rep from * to end.
Row 2: P2, *K2, P2, rep from * to end.
These 2 rows form rib.
Cont in rib for a further 7 rows, ending with **WS** facing for next row.
Row 10 (WS): Rib 2 [4: 1: 3], M1, *rib 6 [6: 7: 7], M1, rep from * to last 2 [4: 2: 4] sts, rib to end.
68 [72: 76: 80] sts.
Change to 4mm (US 6) needles.
Beg and ending rows as indicated and using the **fairisle** technique as described on the information page and repeating the 34 row patt repeat throughout, cont in patt from chart, which is worked entirely in st st beg with a K row, as folls:
Cont in patt until back meas 18 [19: 21: 22] cm, ending with RS facing for next row.
Shape armholes
Keeping chart correct, cast off 4 sts at beg of next 2 rows. 60 [64: 68: 72] sts.
Dec 1 st at each end of next 3 rows, then on foll 2 alt rows. 50 [54: 58: 62] sts.
Cont straight until armhole meas 13 [14: 14: 15] cm, ending with RS facing for next row.

Shape shoulders and back neck
Next row (RS): Cast off 5 [6: 6: 7] sts, patt until there are 7 [7: 8: 8] sts on right needle and turn, leaving rem sts on a holder.
Work each side of neck separately.
Dec 1 st at neck edge on next row.
Cast off rem 6 [6: 7: 7] sts.
With RS facing, rejoin yarns to rem sts, cast off centre 26 [28: 30: 32] sts, patt to end.
Complete to match first side, reversing shapings.

FRONT
Work as given for back to beg of armhole shaping.
Shape armhole and divide for neck
Next row (RS): Cast off 4 sts, patt until there are 29 [31: 33: 35] sts on right needle and turn, leaving rem sts on a holder.
Work each side of neck separately.
Work 1 row.
Dec 1 st at armhole edge on next 3 rows, then on foll 2 alt rows **and at same time** dec 1 st at neck edge on next and every foll alt row.
20 [22: 24: 26] sts.
Dec 1 st at neck edge **only** on 2nd and foll 6 [7: 9: 9] alt rows, then on every foll 4th row until 11 [12: 13: 14] sts rem.
Cont straight until front matches back to beg of

shoulder shaping, ending with RS facing for next row.
Shape shoulder
Cast off 5 [6: 6: 7] sts at beg of next row.
Work 1 row.
Cast off rem 6 [6: 7: 7] sts.
With RS facing, rejoin yarn to rem sts, K2tog and slip this st onto a holder, patt to end. Cast off 4 sts at beg of next row. 29 [31: 33: 35] sts. Complete to match first side, reversing shapings.

MAKING UP
Press as described on the information page.
Join both shoulder seams using back stitch, or mattress stitch if preferred.
Neckband
With RS facing, using 3¼mm (US 3) circular needle and yarn A, pick up and knit 36 [40: 44: 48] sts down left side of neck, K st left on holder and mark this st with a coloured thread, pick up and knit 36 [40: 44: 48] sts up right side of neck, then 22 [26: 26: 30] sts from back.
95 [107: 115: 127] sts.
Round 1 (RS): *K2, P2, rep from * to within 4 sts of marked st, K2, K2tog tbl, K marked st, K2tog, **K2, P2, rep from ** to end.
This row sets position of rib.
Keeping rib correct, cont as folls:

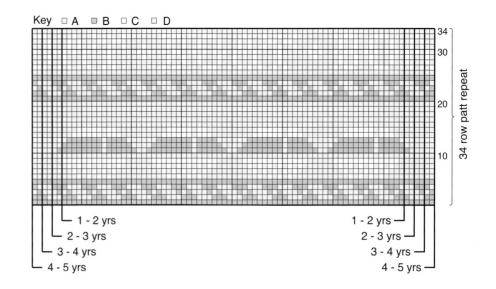

Key ☐ A ▨ B ☐ C ☐ D

1 - 2 yrs
2 - 3 yrs
3 - 4 yrs
4 - 5 yrs

1 - 2 yrs
2 - 3 yrs
3 - 4 yrs
4 - 5 yrs

34 row patt repeat

Round 2: Rib to within 2 sts of marked st, K2tog tbl, K marked st, K2tog, rib to end.

Rep last round twice more. 87 [99: 107: 119] sts.

Cast off in rib, still dec either side of marked st as before.

Armhole borders (both alike)

With RS facing, using 3¼mm (US 3) needles and yarn A, pick up and knit 62 [66: 70: 74] sts evenly all round armhole edge.

Work in rib as given for back for 4 rows, ending with **WS** facing for next row.

Cast off in rib (on **WS**).

See information page for finishing instructions.

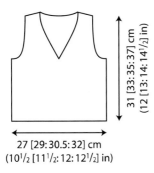

31 [33:35:37] cm
(12 [13: 14: 14½] in)

27 [29:30.5:32] cm
(10½ [11½: 12: 12½] in)

YARN

	1-2	2-3	3-4	4-5	years
To fit chest	56	58	61	64	cm
	22	23	24	25	in

RYC Cashsoft Baby DK

	9	9	10	10	x 50gm

(photographed in Borage 806)

NEEDLES

1 pair 3¼mm (no 10) (US 3) needles
1 pair 3¾mm (no 9) (US 5) needles
3¼mm (no 10) (US 3) circular needle

BUTTONS – 6 x 00319

TENSION

24 sts and 35 rows to 10 cm measured over moss stitch using 3¾mm (US 5) needles.

BACK

Using 3¾mm (US 5) needles cast on 79 [87: 95: 103] sts.
Row 1 (RS): P1, *K1, P1, rep from * to end.
Row 2: Cast on 7 sts, work across these 7 sts as folls: K1, (P1, K1) 3 times, then P1, *K1, P1, rep from * to end.
These 2 rows set position of moss st.
Keeping moss st correct, cont as folls:
Cast on 7 sts at beg of next 9 rows.
149 [157: 165: 173] sts.
Work 5 rows, ending with RS facing for next row.
Dec 1 st at each end of next and every foll 4th row until 79 [83: 87: 91] sts rem, then on foll 0 [0: 0: 1] alt row. 79 [83: 87: 89] sts.
Work 3 [3: 3: 1] rows, ending with RS facing for next row.
Shape back neck
Next row (RS): Work 2 tog, moss st 25 [26: 27: 27] sts and turn, leaving rem sts on a holder.
Work each side of neck separately.
Dec 1 st at neck edge on next 12 rows, then on foll 4 alt rows **and at same time** dec 1 st at side seam edge on 4th [4th: 2nd: 2nd] and 1 [0: 0: 0] foll 4th rows, then on every foll alt row. 2 sts.
Work 1 row, ending with RS facing for next row.
Next row (RS): Work 2 tog and fasten off.
With RS facing, rejoin yarn to rem sts, cast off centre 25 [27: 29: 31] sts, moss st to last 2 sts,

work 2 tog.
Complete to match first side, reversing shapings.

LEFT FRONT

Using 3¾mm (US 5) needles cast on 40 [44: 48: 52] sts.
Row 1 (RS): *P1, K1, rep from * to end.
Row 2: *K1, P1, rep from * to end.
These 2 rows set position of moss st.
Keeping moss st correct, cont as folls:
Cast on 7 sts at beg of next and foll 4 alt rows.
75 [79: 83: 87] sts.
Work 5 rows, ending with RS facing for next row.
Dec 1 st at beg of next and every foll 4th row until 72 [75: 78: 81] sts rem.
Work 1 row, ending with RS facing for next row.
Place hand opening
Next row (RS): Moss st 39 [41: 43: 45] sts and turn, leaving rem sts on a holder.
Work on this set of sts for side section.
Dec 1 st at beg of 2nd and every foll 4th row until 29 [31: 33: 35] sts rem.
Work 2 rows, ending with **WS** facing for next row.
Break yarn and leave sts on a second holder.
With RS facing, rejoin yarn to 33 [34: 35: 36] sts left on first holder and work in moss st for 41 rows for centre front section, ending with **WS** facing for next row.
Join sections
Next row (WS): Moss st 33 [34: 35: 36] sts of centre front section, then moss st across 29 [31: 33: 35] sts left on second holder.
62 [65: 68: 71] sts.
Dec 1 st at beg of next and every foll 4th row until 41 [43: 45: 47] sts rem, ending with **WS** facing for next row.
Shape neck
Keeping moss st correct, cast off 11 [12: 13: 14] sts at beg of next row, then 3 sts at beg of foll 2 alt rows **and at same time** dec 1 st at side seam edge on 4th [4th: 4th: 2nd] and foll 0 [0: 0: 1] alt row. 23 [24: 25: 25] sts.
Dec 1 st at neck edge on next 5 rows, then on foll 4 alt rows, then on 2 foll 4th rows **and at same time** dec 1 st at side seam edge on 3rd [3rd: next: next] and 1 [0: 0: 0] foll 4th row, then on every foll alt row. 3 sts.
Work 3 rows, dec 1 st at side seam edge on 2nd

of these rows and ending with RS facing for next row.
Next row (RS): Work 2 tog and fasten off.

RIGHT FRONT

Using 3¾mm (US 5) needles cast on 40 [44: 48: 52] sts.
Row 1 (RS): *K1, P1, rep from * to end.
Row 2: Cast on 7 sts, work across these 7 sts as folls: K1, (P1, K1) 3 times, *P1, K1, rep from * to end.
These 2 rows set position of moss st.
Keeping moss st correct, cont as folls:
Cast on 7 sts at beg of 2nd and foll 3 alt rows.
75 [79: 83: 87] sts.
Work 6 rows, ending with RS facing for next row.
Dec 1 st at end of next and every foll 4th row until 72 [75: 78: 81] sts rem.
Work 1 row, ending with RS facing for next row.
Place hand opening
Next row (RS): Moss st 33 [34: 35: 36] sts and turn, leaving rem sts on a holder.
Work 40 rows on this set of sts for centre front section, ending with **WS** facing for next row.
Break yarn and leave sts on a second holder.
With RS facing, rejoin yarn to 39 [41: 43: 45] sts left on first holder for side section and moss st to end.
Dec 1 st at end of 2nd and every foll 4th row until 29 [31: 33: 35] sts rem.
Work 2 rows, ending with **WS** facing for next row.
Join sections
Next row (WS): Moss st 29 [31: 33: 35] sts of side section, then moss st across 33 [34: 35: 36] sts left on second holder. 62 [65: 68: 71] sts.
Complete to match left front, reversing shapings.

MAKING UP

Press as described on the information page.
Join both side seams using back stitch, or mattress stitch if preferred.
Yoke
With RS facing and using 3¼mm (US 3) needles, beg and ending at front opening edges, pick up and knit 42 [43: 44: 45] sts up right side of neck, 71 [73: 75: 77] sts from back, then 42 [43: 44: 45] sts down left side of neck. 155 [159: 163: 167] sts.
Row 1 (WS): K3, *P1, K3, rep from * to end.
Row 2: P3, *K1, P3, rep from * to end.

Rows 3 to 12: As rows 1 and 2, 5 times.
Row 13 (WS): K1, K2tog, *P1, K1, K2tog, rep from * to end. 116 [119: 122: 125] sts.
Row 14: P2, *K1, P2, rep from * to end.
Row 15: K2, *P1, K2, rep from * to end.
Rows 16 to 25: As rows 14 and 15, 5 times.
Row 26 (WS): P2tog, *K1, P2tog, rep from * to end. 77 [79: 81: 83] sts.
Row 27: K1, *P1, K1, rep from * to end.
Row 28: P1, *K1, P1, rep from * to end.
Last 2 rows form rib.
Work in rib for a further 4 rows, ending with **WS** facing for next row.
Next row (WS): Rib 10 [8: 6: 4], M1, *rib 3, M1, rep from * to last 10 [8: 6: 4] sts, rib to end. 97 [101: 105: 109] sts.
Shape hood
Change to 3¾mm (US 5) needles.
Row 1 (RS): K1, *P1, K1, rep from * to end.
Row 2: As row 1.
These 2 rows form moss st.
Place marker on centre st of last row.
Next row (RS): Moss st to marked st, M1, moss st marked st, M1, moss st to end.
Work 3 rows.
Rep last 4 rows twice more, then first of these rows (the inc row) again. 105 [109: 113: 117] sts.
Cont straight until hood meas 20 [21: 22: 23] cm, ending with RS facing for next row.
Next row (RS): Moss st to within 2 sts of marked st, K2tog tbl, moss st marked st, K2tog, moss st to end.
Work 1 row.
Rep last 2 rows once more, then first of these rows (the dec row) again.
99 [103: 107: 111] sts.

Next row (WS): Moss st to within 1 st of marked st, P2tog, moss to end. 98 [102: 106: 110] sts.
Next row: Moss st 49 [51: 53: 55] sts and turn.
Fold hood in half with RS facing and, using a spare 3¾mm (US 5) needle, cast off both sets of sts together, taking one st from first needle tog with corresponding st from second needle.
Hem edging
With RS facing and using 3¼mm (US 3) circular needle, beg and ending at front opening edges, pick up and knit 81 [85: 89: 93] sts from lower edge of left front, 163 [171: 179: 187] sts from lower edge of back, then 81 [85: 89: 93] sts from lower edge of right front. 325 [341: 357: 373] sts.
Work in g st for 2 rows, ending with **WS** facing for next row.
Cast off knitwise (on **WS**).
Button band
Using 3¼mm (US 3) needles cast on 7 sts.
Work in g st until band, when slightly stretched, fits up left front opening edge, from cast-off edge of hem edging to beg of hood, ending with **WS** facing for next row.
Cast off knitwise (on **WS**).
Slip st band in place.
Mark positions for 6 buttons on this band – first to come 10 cm up from lower edge, last to come 1 cm below cast-off edge, and rem 4 buttons evenly spaced between.
Buttonhole band
Using 3¼mm (US 3) needles cast on 7 sts.
Work in g st until band, when slightly stretched, fits up right front opening edge, from cast-off edge of hem edging to beg of hood, ending with **WS** facing for next row and with the addition of 6 buttonholes worked to correspond with

positions marked for buttons as folls:
Buttonhole row (RS): K2, K2tog, yfwd, K3.
When band is complete, cast off knitwise (on **WS**).
Slip st band in place.
Hood edging
With RS facing and using 3¼mm (US 3) needles, pick up and knit 120 [124: 128: 132] sts evenly along front edge of hood, between cast-off edges of bands.
Work in g st for 2 rows, ending with **WS** facing for next row.
Cast off knitwise (on **WS**).
Sew ends of edging to top of bands.
Hand opening edgings (all 4 alike)
With RS facing and using 3¼mm (US 3) needles, pick up and knit 33 sts evenly along one row-end edge of one hand opening.
Cast off knitwise (on **WS**).
Join ends of edgings at top and lower edges of openings.
See information page for finishing instructions.

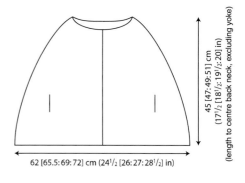

45 [47: 49: 51] cm
(17½ [18½: 19½: 20] in)
(length to centre back neck, excluding yoke)

62 [65.5: 69: 72] cm (24½ [26: 27: 28½] in)

Bo-peep

YARN

	1-2	2-3	3-4	4-5	years
To fit chest	56	58	61	64	cm
	22	23	24	25	in

RYC Cashsoft Baby DK

A Borage	806	2	2	2	2	x 50gm
B Pixie	807	2	2	2	3	x 50gm
C Horseradish	801	2	2	2	3	x 50gm

NEEDLES

1 pair 3¼mm (no 10) (US 3) needles
1 pair 4mm (no 8) (US 6) needles
3¼mm (no 10) (US 3) circular needle

BUTTONS – approx 220 [240: 280: 310] assorted buttons

TENSION

22 sts and 30 rows to 10 cm measured over stocking stitch using 4mm (US 6) needles.

BACK

Using 3¼mm (US 3) needles and yarn A cast on 71 [75: 79: 83] sts.
Work in g st for 4 rows, ending with RS facing for next row.
Change to 4mm (US 6) needles.
Beg with a K row and joining in colours as required, cont in st st in stripes as folls:
Using yarn B, work 5 rows.
Using yarn A, work 1 row.
Using yarn C, work 5 rows.
Using yarn A, work 1 row.
These 12 rows form striped st st.
Cont in striped st st until back meas 18 [19: 21: 24] cm, ending with RS facing for next row.
Shape raglan armholes
Keeping stripes correct, cast off 4 sts at beg of next 2 rows.
63 [67: 71: 75] sts.
Dec 1 st at each end of next 5 rows, then on every foll alt row until 19 [21: 23: 25] sts rem.
Work 1 row, ending with RS facing for next row.
Cast off.

LEFT FRONT

Using 3¼mm (US 3) needles and yarn A cast on 36 [38: 40: 42] sts.

Work in g st for 4 rows, ending with RS facing for next row.
Change to 4mm (US 6) needles.
Beg with a K row and joining in colours as required, cont in striped st st as given for back until 10 rows less have been worked than on back to beg of raglan armhole shaping, ending with RS facing for next row.
Shape front slope
Keeping stripes correct, dec 1 st at end of next and foll 0 [0: 1: 2] alt rows, then on 2 [2: 1: 1] foll 4th rows.
33 [35: 37: 38] sts.
Work 1 [1: 3: 1] rows, ending with RS facing for next row.
Shape raglan armhole
Keeping stripes correct, cast off 4 sts at beg and dec 0 [0: 1: 0] st at end of next row.
29 [31: 32: 34] sts.
Work 1 row.
Dec 1 st at raglan armhole edge of next 5 rows, then on foll 13 [14: 15: 16] alt rows **and at same time** dec 1 st at front slope edge on next [next: 3rd: next] and every foll 4th row.
3 sts.
Work 3 rows, dec 1 st at raglan armhole edge on 2nd of these rows.
Next row (RS): K2tog and fasten off.

RIGHT FRONT

Work to match left front, reversing shapings.

SLEEVES

Using 3¼mm (US 3) needles and yarn A cast on 39 [41: 43: 45] sts.
Work in g st for 4 rows, ending with RS facing for next row.
Change to 4mm (US 6) needles.
Beg with a K row and 1 row using yarn A and then 5 rows using yarn C, cont in striped st st as given for back, shaping sides by inc 1 st at each end of 5th and every foll 4th row to 63 [59: 59: 55] sts, then on every foll – [6th: 6th: 6th] row until there are – [65: 67: 69] sts.
Cont straight until sleeve meas approx 20 [22: 24: 27] cm, ending after same stripe row as on back to beg of raglan armhole shaping and with RS facing for next row.

Shape raglan

Keeping stripes correct, cast off 4 sts at beg of next 2 rows. 55 [57: 59: 61] sts.
Dec 1 st at each end of next 5 rows, then on every foll alt row until 17 sts rem.
Work 1 row, ending with RS facing for next row.
Left sleeve only
Dec 1 st at each end of next row, then cast off 3 sts at beg of foll row. 12 sts.
Dec 1 st at beg of next row, then cast off 3 sts at beg of foll row. 8 sts.
Right sleeve only
Cast off 4 sts at beg and dec 1 st at end of next row. 12 sts.
Work 1 row.
Cast off 3 sts at beg and dec 1 st at end of next row. 8 sts.
Work 1 row.
Both sleeves
Rep last 2 rows once more.
Cast off rem 4 sts.

MAKING UP

Press as described on the information page.
Join raglan seams using back stitch, or mattress stitch if preferred.
Front band
With RS facing, using 3¼mm (US 3) circular needle and yarn A, beg and ending at cast-on edges, pick up and knit 34 [36: 40: 47] sts up right front opening edge to beg of front slope shaping, 36 [38: 38: 40] sts up right front slope, 11 sts from right sleeve, 19 [21: 23: 25] sts from back, 11 sts from left sleeve, 36 [38: 38: 40] sts down left front slope to beg of front slope shaping, then 34 [36: 40: 47] sts down left front opening edge.
181 [191: 201: 221] sts.
Work in g st for 4 rows, ending with **WS** facing for next row.
Cast off knitwise (on **WS**).
See information page for finishing instructions.
Decoration
Using yarn C, embroider a line of french knots centrally onto first stripe in yarn B of back and fronts.
Using photograph as a guide, attach buttons along next stripe in yarn C.

Using yarn A, embroider a line of cross st over next stripe in yarn B.
Using yarn B, embroider a line of cross st over next stripe in yarn C.
Cont in this way, repeating these 4 lines of decoration, over entire back, fronts and sleeves.
For ties, make 2 twisted or crochet cords using yarn A, each 20 cm long, and attach to inside of front band level with beg of front slope shaping.

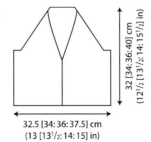

32 [34: 36: 40] cm
(12½ [13½: 14: 15½] in)

32.5 [34: 36: 37.5] cm
(13 [13½: 14: 15] in)

20 [22: 24: 27] cm
(8 [8½: 9½: 10½] in)

Polly

YARN

	1-2	2-3	3-4	4-5	years
To fit chest	56	58	61	64	cm
	22	23	24	25	in

RYC Cashcotton DK

| | 3 | 3 | 3 | 4 | x 50gm |

(photographed in Framboise 614)

NEEDLES

1 pair 3¼mm (no 10) (US 3) needles
1 pair 4mm (no 8) (US 6) needles
3¼mm (no 10) (US 3) circular needle

TENSION

22 sts and 30 rows to 10 cm measured over
stocking stitch using 4mm (US 6) needles.

BACK

Using 3¼mm (US 3) needles cast on 53 [57:
61: 65] sts.
Work in g st for 2 rows, ending with RS facing for
next row. Change to 4mm (US 6) needles.
Beg with a K row, cont in st st, inc 1 st at each
end of 3rd and every foll 4th [6th: 6th: 8th] row to
59 [67: 65: 75] sts, then on every foll 6th [-: 8th: -]
row until there are 63 [-: 71: -] sts.
Work 5 rows, ending with RS facing for next row.
(Back should meas 10 [11: 13: 14] cm.)
Shape armholes
Cast off 4 sts at beg of next 2 rows.
55 [59: 63: 67] sts.
Dec 1 st at each end of next 3 rows.
49 [53: 57: 61] sts.
Cont straight until armhole meas 13 [14: 14: 15] cm,
ending with RS facing for next row.
Shape shoulders and back neck
Next row (RS): Cast off 6 [7: 7: 8] sts, K until
there are 8 [8: 9: 9] sts on right needle and turn,
leaving rem sts on a holder.

Work each side of neck separately.
Dec 1 st at neck edge on next row.
Cast off rem 7 [7: 8: 8] sts.
With RS facing, rejoin yarn to rem sts, cast off
centre 21 [23: 25: 27] sts, K to end.
Complete to match first side, reversing shapings.

LEFT FRONT

Using 3¼mm (US 3) needles cast on 93 [95:
97: 99] sts.
Work in g st for 2 rows, ending with RS facing for
next row. Change to 4mm (US 6) needles.
Beg with a K row, cont in st st as folls:
Work 5 rows, inc 1 st at beg of 3rd of these rows
and ending with **WS** facing for next row.
94 [96: 98: 100] sts.
Shape tie
Cast off 38 sts at beg of next row, then 4 sts at
beg of foll 4 alt rows, ending with RS facing for
next row, **and at same time** inc 1 st at beg of
2nd [4th: 4th: 6th] and foll 4th [0: 0: 0] row.
42 [43: 45: 47] sts.
Shape front slope
Dec 1 st at end of next row and at same edge on
foll 8 rows, then on foll 2 [4: 7: 8] alt rows **and at
same time** inc 1 st at beg of 3rd [next: 3rd: 5th]
and 1 [2: 2: 2] foll 6th [6th: 8th: 8th] rows.
33 [33: 32: 33] sts.
Work 1 row, ending with RS facing for next row.
(Left front should now match back to beg of
armhole shaping.)
Shape armhole
Cast off 4 sts at beg and dec 1 [1: 1: 0] st at end of
next row. 28 [28: 27: 29] sts.
Work 1 row.
Dec 1 st at armhole edge on next 3 rows **and at
same time** dec 1 st at front slope edge on next
and foll 7 [4: 0: 0] alt rows, then on every foll 4th
row until 13 [14: 15: 16] sts rem.

Cont straight until left front matches back to beg
of shoulder shaping, ending with RS facing for
next row.
Shape shoulder
Cast off 6 [7: 7: 8] sts at beg of next row.
Work 1 row.
Cast off rem 7 [7: 8: 8] sts.

RIGHT FRONT

Using 3¼mm (US 3) needles cast on 93 [95:
97: 99] sts.
Work in g st for 2 rows, ending with RS facing for
next row. Change to 4mm (US 6) needles.
Beg with a K row, cont in st st as folls:
Work 4 rows, inc 1 st at end of 3rd of these rows
and ending with RS facing for next row.
94 [96: 98: 100] sts.
Shape tie
Cast off 38 sts at beg of next row, then 4 sts at
beg of foll 4 alt rows **and at same time** inc 1 st at
end of 3rd [5th: 5th: 7th] and foll 4th [0: 0: 0] row.
42 [43: 45: 47] sts.
Work 1 row, ending with RS facing for next row.
Complete to match left front from beg of front
slope shaping, reversing shapings.

SLEEVES

Using 3¼mm (US 3) needles and cast on 45 [49:
49: 53] sts.
Work in g st for 2 rows, ending with RS facing for
next row. Change to 4mm (US 6) needles.
Beg with a K row, cont in st st, shaping sides by
inc 1 st at each end of next and foll 6 alt rows.
59 [63: 63: 67] sts.
Cont straight until sleeve meas 6 cm, ending with
RS facing for next row.
Shape top
Cast off 4 sts at beg of next 2 rows.
51 [55: 55: 59] sts.

Dec 1 st at each end of next and foll 2 alt rows, then on foll row, ending with RS facing for next row. Cast off rem 43 [47: 47: 51] sts.

MAKING UP
Press as described on the information page.
Join both shoulder seams using back stitch, or mattress stitch if preferred.
Front band
With RS facing and using 3¼mm (US 3) circular needle, beg and ending at beg of tie shaping, pick up and knit 38 sts along first set of tie cast-off sts, 66 [71: 76: 81] sts up right front slope, 22 [24: 26: 28] sts from back, 66 [71: 76: 81] sts down left front slope to first set of tie cast-off sts,

then 38 sts along first set of tie cast-off sts. 230 [242: 254: 266] sts.
Row 1 (WS): Knit.
Now work picot cast-off as folls: cast off 2 sts, *slip st now on right needle back onto left needle,

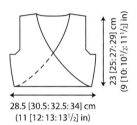

23 [25: 27: 29] cm
(9 [10: 10½: 11½] in)

28.5 [30.5: 32.5: 34] cm
(11 [12: 13: 13½] in)

cast on 2 sts, cast off 4 sts, rep from * to end and fasten off.
See information page for finishing instructions, setting in sleeves using the shallow set-in method.

6 cm
(2½ in)

🧶 ⋮ **Jelly beanie**

YARN

Width around head

33	37	41	45	cm
13	14½	16	17½	in

RYC Cashsoft Baby DK

1	1	1	2	x 50gm

(photographed in Pixie 807 and Chicory 804)

NEEDLES

1 pair 4mm (no 8) (US 6) needles

TENSION

22 sts and 30 rows to 10 cm measured over stocking stitch using 4mm (US 6) needles.

HAT

Using 4mm (US 6) needles cast on 73 [82: 91: 100] sts.

Beg with a K row, cont in st st until hat meas 10 [11: 12: 13] cm, **allowing first few rows to roll to RS** and ending with RS facing for next row.

Shape crown

Row 1 (RS): K1, *K2tog, K6 [7: 8: 9], rep from * to end. 64 [73: 82: 91] sts.

Work 1 row.

Row 3: K1, *K2tog, K5 [6: 7: 8], rep from * to end.

55 [64: 73: 82] sts.

Work 1 row.

Row 5: K1, *K2tog, K4 [5: 6: 7], rep from * to end. 46 [55: 64: 73] sts.

Work 1 row.

Cont in this way, working one less st between decreases on next and every foll alt row until the foll row has been worked:

Next row (RS): K1, *K2tog, K1, rep from * to end. 19 sts.

Work 1 row.

Break yarn and thread through rem 19 sts. Pull up tight and fasten off securely.

TAB

Using 4mm (US 6) needles cast on 15 sts.

Work in g st for 3 rows, ending with **WS** facing for next row.

Cast off knitwise (on **WS**).

MAKING UP

Press as described on the information page.

Join back seam using back stitch, or mattress stitch if preferred, reversing seam for roll at lower edge. Fold tab in half and attach row-end edges to top of crown.

![yarn icon] :

Wiggly scarf

YARN

RYC Cashsoft Baby DK

A Pixie	807	2	x 50gm
B Cloud	805	2	x 50gm

NEEDLES

1 pair 4mm (no 8) (US 6) needles

FINISHED SIZE

Completed scarf measures 13 cm (5 in) wide and 122 cm (48 in) long.

TENSION

22 sts and 30 rows to 10 cm measured over stocking stitch using 4mm (US 6) needles.

FIRST SECTION

Using 4mm (US 6) needles and yarn A cast on 38 sts.
Row 1 (WS): Using yarn A, purl.
Row 2: Using yarn A, K1, (inc in next st, K3, sl 1, K1, psso, K2tog, K3, inc in next st) 3 times, K1.
Rows 3 and 4: As rows 1 and 2.
Rows 5 to 8: Using yarn B, as rows 1 and 2, twice.
These 8 rows form patt.
Cont in patt until first section meas approx 61 cm, ending after patt row 4 and with RS facing for next row.**
Break yarn and leave sts on a holder.

SECOND SECTION

Work as given for first section to **.
Join sections
Holding sections with RS together, cast off all sts tog, taking one st from first section tog with corresponding st of second section.

MAKING UP

Press as described on the information page.
Make six 2.5 cm diameter pompoms using yarn B and attach to points of cast-on edges as in photograph.

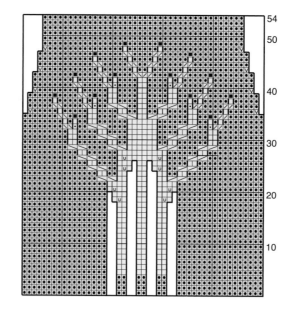

Apple tree blanket

YARN
RYC Cashsoft Baby DK

7   x 50gm

(photographed in Chicory 804)

NEEDLES
1 pair 3¼mm (no 10) (US 3) needles
1 pair 4mm (no 8) (US 6) needles
Cable needle

FINISHED SIZE
Completed blanket measures 61 cm (24 in) wide
and 94 cm (37 in) long.

TENSION
22 sts and 30 rows to 10 cm measured over
stocking stitch using 4mm (US 6) needles.

SPECIAL ABBREVIATIONS
Cr4R = slip next st onto cable needle and leave at
back of work, K3, then P1 from cable needle;
Cr4L = slip next 3 sts onto cable needle and
leave at front of work, P1, then K3 from cable
needle; **Cr2R** = slip next st onto cable needle and
leave at back of work, K1, then P1 from cable
needle; **Cr2L** = slip next st onto cable needle and
leave at front of work, P1, then K1 from cable
needle; **MB** = (K1, P1, K1, P1, K1) all into next st,
turn, P5, turn, sl 1, K1, psso, K1, K2tog, turn, P3,
turn, slip 2 sts, K1, pass 2 slipped sts over.

Pattern note: The number of sts varies whilst
working chart. Chart begins with 40 sts,
increases to 48 sts, and then decreases back
down to 40 sts.

BLANKET
Using 3¼mm (US 3) needles cast on 134 sts.
Work in g st for 8 rows, ending with RS facing for
next row.
Change to 4mm (US 6) needles.
Row 1 (RS): K7, work next 40 sts as row 1 of
chart, K40, work next 40 sts as row 1 of chart, K7.
Row 2: K7, work next 40 sts as row 2 of chart,
P40, work next 40 sts as row 2 of chart, K7.
These 2 rows set the sts.
Cont as set until all 54 rows of chart have been
completed.
Row 55 (RS): K47, work next 40 sts as row 1 of
chart, K47.

Row 56: K7, P40, work next 40 sts as row 2 of
chart, P40, K7.
These 2 rows set the sts.
Cont as set until all 54 rows of chart have been
completed.
Rep last 108 rows once more, then rows 1 to 54
again, ending with RS facing for next row.
Change to 3¼mm (US 3) needles.
Work in g st for 7 rows, ending with **WS** facing for
next row.
Cast off knitwise (on **WS**).

MAKING UP
Press as described on the information page.

Key
☐ K on RS,
P on WS

▣ P on RS,
K on WS

⊍ M1

⧄ Cr4R

⧅ Cr4L

⧄ Cr2R

⧅ Cr2L

⊡ K1 tbl

▩ MB

☒ K2tog

▢ no stitch

YARN
RYC Cashsoft Baby DK

1   x 50gm

(photographed in Pixie 807)

NEEDLES
1 pair 4mm (no 8) (US 6) needles

FINISHED SIZE
Completed cat stands approx 16 cm (6¼ in) tall.

EXTRAS – Oddments of lilac and cream yarn for embroidery. 40 cm length of narrow satin ribbon in each of pink and blue. Washable toy filling.

TENSION
22 sts and 30 rows to 10 cm measured over stocking stitch using 4mm (US 6) needles.

FIRST SIDE (worked downwards, starting at tip of tail)
Using 4mm (US 6) needles cast on 4 sts.
Beg with a K row, work in st st throughout as folls:
Inc 1 st at end of 4th row and at same edge on foll 3rd row, then on foll alt row, ending with **WS** facing for next row. 7 sts.
Dec 1 st at beg of next and 2 foll alt rows **and at same time** inc 1 st at end of next row and at same edge on foll 4 rows, ending with RS facing for next row. 9 sts.
Cast on 22 sts (for top of back) at beg of next row. 31 sts.
Dec 1 st at beg of next row and at same edge on foll 2 rows. 28 sts.
Work 7 rows, ending with **WS** facing for next row.
Dec 1 st at end of next and foll alt row. 26 sts.
Work 2 rows, ending with RS facing for next row.
Inc 1 st at beg of next and foll alt row, ending with **WS facing for next row. 28 sts.
Divide for legs
Next row (WS): P9 and slip these sts onto a holder for back leg, cast off next 3 sts, P to end.

Work on this set of 16 sts only for front leg.
Row 1 (RS): K to last 2 sts, K2tog. 15 sts.
Row 2: P2tog, P to last st, inc in last st.
Row 3: As row 1. 14 sts.
Row 4: P3tog, P to last st, inc in last st. 13 sts.
Row 5: As row 1. 12 sts.
Row 6: P3tog, P to end. 10 sts.
Row 7: As row 1. 9 sts.
Row 8: P2tog, P to last 2 sts, P2tog.
Cast off rem 7 sts.
Shape back leg
With RS facing, rejoin yarn to rem 9 sts and cont as folls:
Row 1 (RS): Knit.
Row 2: Purl.
Row 3: Inc in first st, K to end. 10 sts.
Row 4: Purl.
Row 5: Inc in first st, K to last 2 sts, K2tog.
Row 6: P3tog, P to end. 8 sts.
Row 7: K to last 2 sts, K2tog. 7 sts.
Row 8: P to last 2 sts, P2tog.
Cast off rem 6 sts.

FIRST UNDERBODY SECTION
Using 4mm (US 6) needles cast on 26 sts.
Beg with a **P** row, work in st st throughout as folls:
Work 1 row, ending with RS facing for next row.
Complete as given for first side from **.

SECOND SIDE AND UNDERBODY SECTIONS
Work as given for first side and underbody section, reversing all shapings by reading K for P and vice versa.

HEAD (make 2 pieces)
Using 4mm (US 6) needles cast on 5 sts.
Beg with a K row, work in st st throughout as folls:
Work 1 row, ending with **WS** facing for next row.
Inc 1 st at each end of next 8 rows. 21 sts.
Work 10 rows, ending with **WS** facing for next row.
Dec 1 st at each end of next and foll 3 alt rows,

then on foll row, ending with **WS** facing for next row.
Cast off rem 11 sts.

OUTER EARS (make 2 pieces)
First piece
Using 4mm (US 6) needles cast on 14 sts.
***Beg with a K row, work in st st throughout as folls:
Work 1 row, ending with **WS** facing for next row.
Dec 1 st at beg of next and every foll alt row until 6 sts rem, then dec 1 st at shaped edge on next 3 rows, ending with **WS** facing for next row.
Next row (WS): P3tog and fasten off.
Second piece
Work as given for first piece, reversing shaping by dec at **END** of rows.

INNER EARS (make 2 pieces)
Using 4mm (US 6) needles cast on 12 sts.
Complete as given for outer ears from ***.

MAKING UP
Do NOT press.
Join underbody pieces along cast-on edges, leaving a small opening. Sew underbody sections to sides, then join rem edges of sides. Insert toy filling and sew opening closed. Join head pieces, leaving cast-on edges open. Insert toy filling, then sew head to body as in photograph. Join inner and outer ears, easing outer ear to fit inner ear and leaving cast-on edges open. Turn RS out, make a pleat in cast-on edges and then sew ears to head as in photograph.
Using photograph as a guide and oddment of lilac yarn, embroider face as folls: Embroider triangular nose in satin st, then mouth in chain st. For eyes, embroider a group of sloping satin sts. Embroider stem st whiskers either side of nose and above eyes. On each leg, embroider 4 straight sts as in photograph to separate toes. Using oddment of cream yarn, embroider french knots at centres of eyes. Tie ribbon around neck.

Derek dog

YARN
RYC Cashsoft Baby DK

1   x 50gm

(photographed in Horseradish 801)

NEEDLES
1 pair 4mm (no 8) (US 6) needles

FINISHED SIZE
Completed dog stands approx 16 cm (6¼ in) tall.

EXTRAS
Oddments of brown and beige yarn for embroidery. 40 cm length of taffeta ribbon. Washable toy filling.

TENSION
22 sts and 30 rows to 10 cm measured over stocking stitch using 4mm (US 6) needles.

FIRST SIDE (worked downwards, starting at tip of tail)
Using 4mm (US 6) needles cast on 9 sts.
Beg with a K row, work in st st throughout as folls:
Work 5 rows, ending with **WS** facing for next row.
Dec 1 st at end of next row. 8 sts.
Cast off 2 sts at beg and inc 1 st at end of next row. 7 sts.
Dec 1 st at end of next row, then inc 1 st at end of foll row. 7 sts.
Work 3 rows, ending with RS facing for next row.
Cast on 24 sts (for top of back) at beg of next row. 31 sts.
Dec 1 st at beg of next row and at same edge on foll 2 rows. 28 sts.
Work 7 rows, ending with **WS** facing for next row.
Dec 1 st at end of next and foll alt row. 26 sts.
Work 2 rows, ending with RS facing for next row.
Inc 1 st at beg of next and foll alt row, ending with **WS facing for next row. 28 sts.
Divide for legs
Next row (WS): P9 and slip these sts onto a holder for back leg, cast off next 3 sts, P to end.

Work on this set of 16 sts only for front leg.
Row 1 (RS): K to last 2 sts, K2tog. 15 sts.
Row 2: P2tog, P to last st, inc in last st.
Row 3: As row 1. 14 sts.
Row 4: P3tog, P to last st, inc in last st. 13 sts.
Row 5: As row 1. 12 sts.
Row 6: P3tog, P to end. 10 sts.
Row 7: As row 1. 9 sts.
Row 8: P2tog, P to last 2 sts, P2tog.
Cast off rem 7 sts.
Shape back leg
With RS facing, rejoin yarn to rem 9 sts and cont as folls:
Row 1 (RS): Knit.
Row 2: Purl.
Row 3: Inc in first st, K to end. 10 sts.
Row 4: Purl.
Row 5: Inc in first st, K to last 2 sts, K2tog.
Row 6: P2tog, P to end. 9 sts.
Row 7: K to last 2 sts, K2tog. 8 sts.
Row 8: P to last 2 sts, P2tog.
Cast off rem 7 sts.

FIRST UNDERBODY SECTION
Using 4mm (US 6) needles cast on 26 sts.
Beg with a **P** row, work in st st throughout as folls:
Work 1 row, ending with RS facing for next row.
Complete as given for first side from **.

SECOND SIDE AND UNDERBODY SECTIONS
Work as given for first side and underbody section, reversing all shapings by reading K for P and vice versa.

HEAD (make 2 pieces)
Using 4mm (US 6) needles cast on 11 sts.
Beg with a K row, work in st st throughout as folls:
Work 2 rows, ending with RS facing for next row.
Inc 1 st at each end of next and foll 2 alt rows. 17 sts.
Work 11 rows, ending with RS facing for next row.

Dec 1 st at each end of next 4 rows, ending with RS facing for next row.
Cast off rem 9 sts.

EARS (make 4 pieces)
Using 4mm (US 6) needles cast on 4 sts.
Beg with a K row, work in st st throughout as folls:
Work 1 row, ending with **WS** facing for next row.
Inc 1 st at each end of next 2 rows, then on foll alt row. 10 sts.
Work 7 rows, ending with RS facing for next row.
Dec 1 st at each end of next and foll alt row, ending with **WS** facing for next row. 6 sts.
Dec 1 st at beg of next row and at same edge on foll 3 rows.
Next row (WS): P2tog and fasten off.
Make another one piece in exactly this way, then make a further 2 pieces, reversing shaping.

MAKING UP
Do NOT press.
Join underbody pieces along cast-on edges, leaving a small opening. Sew underbody sections to sides, then join rem edges of sides. Insert toy filling and sew opening closed. Join head pieces, leaving cast-on edges open. Insert toy filling, then sew head to body as in photograph. Join pairs of ear pieces, leaving cast-on edges open. Turn RS out, and then sew ears to head as in photograph.
Using photograph as a guide and oddment of beige yarn, embroider face as folls: Embroider triangular nose in chain st, then mouth in back st. For eyes, embroider outline in back st, then fill in eye with satin st. Using oddment of brown yarn, embroider back st whiskers either side of nose and above eyes. Work centres of eyes as satin st using oddment of brown yarn, then embroider french knots at centres of eyes using main colour. On each leg, embroider 4 straight sts using oddment of brown yarn as in photograph to separate toes. Tie ribbon around neck.

Daphne duck

YARN
RYC Cashsoft Baby DK

A Limone	802	1	x 50gm
B Imp	803	1	x 50gm

NEEDLES
1 pair 4mm (no 8) (US 6) needles

FINISHED SIZE
Completed duck is approx 32 cm (12½ in) from tip of tail to tip of beak.

EXTRAS
EXTRAS – Oddment of grey yarn for embroidery. Washable toy filling.

TENSION
22 sts and 30 rows to 10 cm measured over stocking stitch using 4mm (US 6) needles.

LEFT SIDE
Using 4mm (US 6) needles and yarn A cast on 36 sts.
Beg with a K row, work in st st throughout as folls:
Inc 1 st at each end of next and foll 5 alt rows. 48 sts.
Work 1 row, ending with RS facing for next row.
Inc 1 st at beg of next and foll 7 alt rows. 56 sts.
Work 1 row, ending with RS facing for next row.
Inc 1 st at beg of next and foll 2 alt rows **and at same time** dec 1 st at end of next and foll 2 alt rows. 56 sts.
Work 1 row, ending with RS facing for next row.
Shape tail
Next row (RS): Inc in first st, K7, K2tog and turn, leaving rem sts on a holder.
Work on these 10 sts only for tail.
Dec 1 st at beg of next row and at same edge on every foll row until 2 sts rem.
Next row (WS): P2tog and fasten off.

Shape upper edge of back
With RS facing, rejoin yarn to rem sts, K2tog, K22, K2tog and turn, leaving rem sts on a holder.
Work on these 24 sts only for upper edge of back.
Dec 1 st at each end of next 2 rows, ending with **WS** facing for next row.
Cast off rem 20 sts purlwise (on **WS**).
Shape head
With RS facing, rejoin yarn to rem sts, inc in first st, K to last 2 sts, K2tog.
Work on these 20 sts for head.
Work 1 row, ending with RS facing for next row.
Inc 1 st at beg of next and foll alt row **and at same time** dec 1 st at end of next and foll alt row. 20 sts.
Work 1 row, ending with RS facing for next row.
Inc 1 st at beg of next and foll alt row **and at same time** inc 1 st at end of next row and at same edge on foll 3 rows. 26 sts.
Dec 1 st at beg of 3rd and foll 4th row. 24 sts.
Work 1 row, ending with RS facing for next row.
Place marker at beg of last row.
Dec 1 st at beg of next and foll 3 alt rows **and at same time** dec 1 st at end of next row and at same edge on foll 7 rows. 12 sts.
Cast off 3 sts at beg of next 2 rows.
Cast off rem 6 sts.

RIGHT SIDE
Work as given for left side, reversing all shapings by reading K for P and vice versa.

GUSSET
Using 4mm (US 6) needles and yarn A cast on 10 sts.
Beg with a K row, work in st st throughout as folls:
Inc 1 st at each end of 5th and every foll 4th row to 20 sts, then on every foll 6th row until there are 24 sts.
Work 23 rows, ending with RS facing for next row.

Dec 1 st at each end of next and foll 6th row, then on every foll 4th row until 12 sts rem.
Work 19 rows, ending with RS facing for next row.
Break off yarn A and join in yarn B.
Work 14 rows, ending with RS facing for next row.
Dec 1 st at each end of next 4 rows.
Cast off rem 4 sts.

TOP BEAK
Join sides together along upper edge, from marker to fasten-off point of tail.
With RS facing, using 4mm (US 6) needles and yarn B, pick up and knit 12 sts along straight row-end edges of head either side of marker.
Beg with a P row, work in st st throughout as folls:
Work 13 rows, ending with RS facing for next row.
Dec 1 st at each end of next 4 rows.
Cast off rem 4 sts.

FEET (make 4 pieces)
Using 4mm (US 6) needles and yarn B cast on 6 sts.
Work in g st, inc 1 st at each end of 5th and foll 5 alt rows. 18 sts.
Work 1 row, ending with RS facing for next row.
Dec 1 st at each end of next 8 rows, ending with RS facing for next row.
Next row (RS): K2tog and fasten off.

MAKING UP
Do NOT press.
Matching beak sections and cast-on edge of gusset to tip of tail, sew gusset to lower edges of sides, leaving an opening. Insert toy filling and sew opening closed. Join pairs of feet pieces, leaving cast-on edges open. Turn RS out, then sew feet to body as in photograph.
Using photograph as a guide and oddment of grey yarn, embroider eyes by working 8 small straight sts radiating out from one point.

 Mr Sleepy Ted

YARN
RYC Cashsoft Baby DK

A	Crocus	808	1	x 50gm
B	Blue Boy	809	1	x 50gm

NEEDLES
1 pair 4mm (no 8) (US 6) needles

FINISHED SIZE
Completed teddy stands approx 27 cm (10½in) tall.

EXTRAS
Oddments of brown and pale blue yarn for embroidery. 3 buttons. Washable toy filling.

TENSION
22 sts and 30 rows to 10 cm measured over stocking stitch using 4mm (US 6) needles.

BODY (make 2 pieces)
First leg
Using 4mm (US 6) needles and yarn B cast on 15 sts.
Work in g st for 24 rows, ending with RS facing for next row.**
Break yarn and leave sts on a holder.
Second leg
Work as given for first leg to **.
Join legs
Next row (RS): K 15 sts of second leg, then K 15 sts of first leg. 30 sts.
Work a further 9 rows, ending with RS facing for next row.
Next row (RS): (K2tog, K3) 6 times.
24 sts.
Work 7 rows.
Next row (RS): (K2, K2tog) 6 times.
18 sts.
Work a further 15 rows, ending with RS facing for next row.
Cast off 3 sts at beg of next 2 rows.
Cast off rem 12 sts.

HEAD
Using 4mm (US 6) needles and yarn A cast on 18 sts.
Work in g st for 60 rows, ending with RS facing for next row.
Cast off.

MUZZLE (make 2 pieces)
Using 4mm (US 6) needles and yarn A cast on 13 sts.
Work in g st for 4 rows, ending with RS facing for next row.
Next row (RS): K1, (K2tog, K2) 3 times. 10 sts.
Work a further 4 rows.
Cast off (on **WS**).

EARS (make 2)
Using 4mm (US 6) needles and yarn A cast on 7 sts.
Work in g st for 3 rows, ending with **WS** facing for next row.
Next row (WS): Inc in first st, K5, inc in last st. 9 sts.
Work 9 rows.
Next row (WS): K2tog, K5, K2tog. 7 sts.
Work 1 row.
Cast off (on **WS**).

ARMS (make 2)
Using 4mm (US 6) needles and yarn A cast on 15 sts.
Work in g st for 5 rows, ending with **WS** facing for next row.
Break off yarn A and join in yarn B.
Work 24 rows, ending with **WS** facing for next row.
Next row (WS): Inc in first st, K13, inc in last st.
17 sts.
Work 3 rows.
Cast off (on **WS**).

FEET (make 2)
Using 4mm (US 6) needles and yarn A cast on 15 sts.

Work in g st for 7 rows, ending with **WS** facing for next row.
Cast off (on **WS**).

TAIL
Using 4mm (US 6) needles and yarn A cast on 7 sts.
Work in g st for 12 rows, ending with RS facing for next row.
Cast off.

MAKING UP
Do NOT press.
Sew body pieces together, leaving cast-off edges open. Insert toy filling and sew cast-off edges closed, gathering up edge. Fold head piece in half and join row-end edges, leaving cast-on and cast-off edges open. Insert toy filling and sew cast-on and cast-off edges closed, gathering up edge. Sew head to body. Sew muzzle pieces together, leaving cast-on edges open. Insert toy filling and sew cast-on edges closed. Sew muzzle to head as in photograph. Make pleat in cast-off edge of ears, then sew this edge to head as in photograph. Fold arms in half and join row-end and cast-on edges, leaving cast-off edge open. Insert toy filling, then sew arms to body. Fold feet in half and join row-end and cast-on edges, leaving cast-off edge open. Insert toy filling, then sew feet to legs. Fold tail in half and join row-end and cast-on edges, leaving cast-off edge open. Sew tail to back of body.
Using photograph as a guide and chain st, embroider outline of pyjama jacket onto body using oddment of pale blue yarn. Attach buttons as in photograph. Using photograph as a guide and using oddment of brown yarn, embroider chain st eyes and mouth and satin st nose onto head and muzzle sections.

BELGIUM
Pavan, Meerlaanstraat 73,
B9860 Balegem (Oosterzele).
Tel: (32) 9 221 8594
Email: pavan@pandora.be

CANADA
Diamond Yarn,
9697 St Laurent,
Montreal,
Quebec, H3L 2N1.
Tel: (514) 388 6188

Diamond Yarn (Toronto),
155 Martin Ross,
Unit 3, Toronto,
Ontario, M3J 2L9.
Tel: (416) 736 6111
Email: diamond@diamondyarn.com
Web: www.diamondyarns.com

FINLAND
Coats Opti Oy,
Ketjutie 3,
04220 Kerava
Tel: (358) 9 274 871
Fax: (358) 9 274 87330
Email: coatsopti.sales@coats.com

FRANCE
Elle Tricot : 8 Rue du Coq,
67000 Strasbourg.
Tel: (33) 3 88 23 03 13.
Email: elletricot@agat.net.
Web: www.elletricote.com

GERMANY
Wolle & Design,
Wolfshovener Strasse 76,
52428 Julich-Stetternich.
Tel: (49) 2461 54735.
Email: Info@wolleunddesign.de
Web: www.wolleunddesign.de

HOLLAND
de Afstap, Oude Leliestraat 12,
1015 AW Amsterdam.
Tel: (31) 20 6231445

HONG KONG
East Unity Co Ltd, Unit B2, 7/F Block B,
Kailey Industrial Centre,
12 Fung Yip Street, Chai Wan.
Tel: (852) 2869 7110
Fax: (852) 2537 6952
Email: eastuni@netvigator.com

ICELAND
Storkurinn, Laugavegi 59,
101 Reykjavik.
Tel: (354) 551 8258
Fax: (354) 562 8252
Email: malin@mmedia.is

ITALY
D.L. srl, Via Piave, 24 – 26,
20016 Pero, Milan.
Tel: (39) 02 339 10 180.

JAPAN
Puppy Co Ltd,
T151-0051,
3-16-5 Sendagaya,
Shibuyaku, Tokyo.
Tel: (81) 3 3490 2827
Email: info@rowan-jaeger.com

KOREA
Coats Korea Co Ltd,
5F Kuckdong B/D,
935-40 Bangbae-Dong,
Seocho-Gu, Seoul.
Tel: (82) 2 521 6262.
Fax: (82) 2 521 5181

NORWAY
Coats Knappehuset A/S,
Postboks 63,
2801 Gjovik.
Tel: (47) 61 18 34 00
Fax: (47) 61 18 34 20

SINGAPORE
Golden Dragon Store,
101 Upper Cross Street #02-51,
People's Park Centre.
Singapore 058357
Tel: (65) 65358454.
Email:gdscraft@hotmail.com

SOUTH AFRICA
Arthur Bales PTY,
PO Box 44644,
Linden 2104.
Tel: (27) 11 888 2401.

SPAIN
Oyambre, Pau Claris 145,
80009 Barcelona.
Tel: (34) 670 011957.
Email: comercial@oyambreonline.com

SWEDEN
Wincent, Norrtullsgatan 65,
113 45 Stockholm.
Tel: (46) 8 33 70 60
Fax: (46) 8 33 70 68
Email: wincent@chello.se
Web: www.wincentyarn.com

TAIWAN
Laiter Wool Knitting Co Ltd,
10-1 313 Lane, Sec 3,
Chung Ching North Road,
Taipei.
Tel: (886) 2 2596 0269.

U.S.A.
Westminster Fibers Inc,
4 Townsend West,
Suite 8, Nashua,
New Hampshire 03063.
Tel: (1 603) 886 5041 / 5043.
Email: rowan@westminsterfibers.com

U.K.
Rowan,
Green Lane Mill,
Holmfirth,
West Yorkshire,
HD9 2DX.
Tel: 01484 681881.
Email: mail@ryclassic.com
Web: www.ryclassic.com

For All Other Countries:
Please contact Rowan for stockists details.

Models – Poppie Lewis, Daisie Lewis,
Georgina Reed, Felix, Brogan,
James Sexton, George Turney
and Tom Ferguson

Styling – Tara Sloggett
Photography – Mark Scott
Hair and Make up – KJ
Design Layout – Nicky Downes

First published in Great Britain in 2006
by Rowan Yarns Ltd, Green Lane Mill,
Holmfirth, West Yorkshire, England, HD9 2DX

British Library Cataloguing in
Publication Data
Rowan Yarns
RYC Bambino
ISBN: 1-904485-66-9